THE
INCOMPARABLE
JESUS

THE INCOMPARABLE JESUS

Grant H. Palmer

Greg Kofford Books
Salt Lake City
2005

2013 12 11   5 4 3   Paperback

For my wife Connie, my children and their spouses: Karl and Jill, Julie and Rob, Rhett and Lisa, Tamara and Tyson.

*And for my grandchildren, Stephanie, Brittany,
Kelcie, Megan, Candace, Alison, Mikelle,
Austin, Dylan, Kristi, and others not yet born.*

Contents

Illustrations

Map

Paintings by Carl Bloch, originals at Frederiksborg Slot (Castle), Hillerod, Denmark. Images provided by HopeGallery.com. Used by permission.

Preface

Among religious founders such as Gautama Buddha, Mohammed, Krishna, Lao-tzu, and all others, Jesus is unique in that his life and mission were predicted long before his birth. But what makes him incomparable are his ideal character and moral teachings, miracles, and promises. Nearly two billion people regard Jesus as "The Way" because, to a lesser or greater degree, he is "manifest" in their lives through his "spirit," "peace," and guiding "truth." Moreover, while others have performed miracles throughout history, Jesus heals people in many dimensions, making them physically, emotionally, socially, and spiritually whole. Finally, he offers us the superior promise of a resurrected body rather than mere immortality of the spirit beyond the grave. Old Testament prophets Isaiah, Zechariah, and Jesus himself predicted his resurrection from the dead. He was seen by nearly two dozen identified witnesses, plus another 500 in the Galilee area. The risen Christ alone offers this incomparable promise and evidence.

This book centers primarily on Jesus the man, his character, personality, and promises to his disciples. Within his teachings, doctrines, parables, and miracles, Jesus reveals *himself*. Specifically, the book identifies what Jesus is like and encourages a practical application of these characteristics in our life. My hope is that this small volume will aid others in their preparation for teaching and speaking in church, and help all readers better "know" Jesus and receive eternal life.

At age seventeen I received a patriarchal blessing, which said in part: "You shall develop a great love in your heart for your fellow men. This love will carry you to the places of those who are wayward, and you will strengthen them and . . . convince people of the truthfulness of Jesus Christ." I was subsequently employed in the Church Educational System of the Church of Jesus Christ of Latter-day Saints for thirty-four years. During the last thirteen years of my career (1988-2001), I was the LDS Institute director at the Salt Lake County Jail. There I worked with adult inmates, and my appointment centered on biblical teaching and counseling. Being the only full-time religious instructor and chaplain, I was requested to teach non-denominational Bible classes suitable for all Christian inmates. During my assignment I came to a new appreciation of the New Testament, especially the four Gospels. The first six chapters represent the teaching outline that I used.

ഓരു

Chapter 1

Knowing Jesus

Over 6.3 billion people currently live on the earth. Almost two billion (33 percent) are Christian and another billion and a half (22–25 percent) follow Islam. Islam is increasing 2.9 percent a year, faster than the 2.3 percent growth in world population. This statistical trend suggests that Islam will likely surpass Christianity within a few decades. Asiatic religions represent another billion and a half (25 percent), comprised mainly of one billion adherents of Hinduism (15 percent), 350 million followers of Buddhism (6 percent), and 225 million adherents of Chinese traditional (4 percent). The nonreligious include the final billion (14 percent). Approximately 4,200 religions publish adherent statistics. Of these 4,200 churches, denominations, religious bodies, faith groups, tribes, cultures and movements, most are Christian.[1]

The overwhelming diversity in Christianity is not found in the behavioral requirements of the different churches—the overriding emphasis of Jesus' teachings—but rather in each denomination's theological and philosophical interpretation of scripture. History clearly teaches us that breakaway movements from existing Christian churches were caused by these inherent doctrinal differences.

The founding people(s) of these new theological movements usually claim to have received strong spiritual impres-
sions or some other form of revelatory confirmation, for their
actions. Revelation, however, is obviously not a very reliable
guide in proving truth. Christian churches differ on many topics, such as the form of God, the nature of humankind, who
may marry and what forms marriage may take, the responsibilities and powers of ecclesiastical leaders, sabbath day issues, the
millennium, additional scripture, the nature of life after death,
family structure in this life and the next, eternal punishment,
who must be baptized and by whom, and a host of other theological matters on which Jesus had little or nothing to say.
Rather, he asks that such "disputations among you concerning
the points of my doctrine" end (3 Ne. 11:28; see also Matt
5:25). It seems clear to me that Jesus desires us to follow his
behavior, not to focus on the distinctive beliefs of our theological systems.

The message of the New Testament to me is that Jesus
is more interested in right actions than in "right beliefs." He
centers on individuals and their behavior. He asks that we come
unto him and partake of his divine nature, challenging us to
conduct an empirical test to determine whether he and his
teachings are of God. Jesus promises in his Sermon on the
Mount, that "whosoever heareth these sayings of mine, and
doeth them, . . . [they are] founded upon a rock," "and that Rock
[is] . . . Christ" (Matt. 7:24; emphasis mine. See also 1 Cor.
10:4). Jesus *is* the Sermon on the Mount. Rather than advocating a controversial metaphysic or a highly subjective methodol-
ogy of "feeling spiritual" by which we may know him and his
teachings, he emphasizes: "If any man will *do* his [the Father's]
will, he shall *know* of the doctrine, whether it be of God, or
whether I speak of myself" (John 7:17; emphasis mine; see also
Matt. 7:21–25).

This is the epistemology of Jesus: To "do" is how one "knows." The Apostle Peter, in his old age, reemphasized this point. He had carefully observed Jesus for three years and knew him well. In one of his two surviving epistles, Peter lists nine personal characteristics for which the Saints ought to strive. He repeatedly referred to them collectively as "the way of truth," "the right way," and "the way of righteousness" and undoubtedly observed them in Jesus during his three-year ministry (2 Pet. 2:2, 15, 21). Jesus displayed "diligence" in revealing his Father's "divine nature," manifested strong "faith" in God, was "virtuous," and demonstrated "knowledge" of the scriptures. He exhibited "temperance" (meaning self-control, moderation, and balance) and "patience" with others. He also demonstrated "godliness" (goodness), "brotherly kindness" (gentleness), and enormous "charity" (love and compassion) for his fellow beings. Peter then explained that when these nine qualities "be in you, and abound" then we have "knowledge of our Lord Jesus Christ." Nine small words but in them reside eternal life!

The four Gospels provide many examples of these qualities during Jesus' three-year ministry, discussed in subsequent chapters. For now, Peter, as leader of the Church, advises all who have faith in Christ to:

> be partakers of the divine nature [of Jesus Christ] and escape the corruption that is in the world . . .
>
> [and by] giving all diligence, add to your faith virtue; and to virtue knowledge;
>
> And to knowledge temperance; and to temperance patience; and to patience godliness;
>
> And to godliness brotherly kindness; and to brotherly kindness charity.
>
> For if these things be in you, and abound, they make you that ye shall neither be barren nor unfruitful in the knowledge of our Lord Jesus Christ. . . .

Give diligence to make your calling and election sure: for if ye do these things, ye shall never fall. (2 Pet. 1:4–9, 10)

Paul also taught the Saints to strive for these characteristics "until Christ be formed in you." His list of the fruits of the spirit by which a Christian is known is almost identical with Peter's. He also lists nine qualities: "love, joy, peace, long-suffering, gentleness, goodness, faith, meekness, temperance" (Gal. 4:19; 5:22-23). Taking upon us the name of Christ and his character, as Jesus said in one of his recorded prayers, is to "*know* thee the only true God, and Jesus Christ, whom thou hast sent" and thus receive "life eternal" (John 17:3; cf. 10:27–28; emphasis mine). Being like Jesus is far more ambitious than saying that we know he lives.

Arthur R. Bassett, a professor of humanities at Brigham Young University, has observed: "One comes to know Jesus by studying *the man himself* rather than *the teachings* he espoused isolated from the facts of his life. My own experience has led me to conclude that we should do more to make Jesus the man a central focal point in our meetings and lessons. Theological principles become much more meaningful when viewed in the context of a life. People inspire us much more than principles do."[2]

There is indeed a critical need to make Jesus Christ himself "a central focal point in our meetings and lessons." Recently the LDS Church has reemphasized the importance of centering our worship in Christ. This emphasis appears in frequent general conference sermons that draw on the life of Christ, but I have not noticed much change at the local level.

Sometimes I think that, by emphasizing the Book of Mormon, we unconsciously send a message that the Bible is inferior. This inadvertent negative result came to my attention several years ago when my twelve-year-old granddaughter asked her mother: "Is it all right to read the Bible in our church?"

The Church is a vehicle to deliver the good news of Jesus Christ; thus, all that we do in our weekly services, especially the preaching and teaching, should be framed around, linked to, and focused on Christ. Is it not in Christ and his teachings alone that we are judged? Focusing on anything less than Jesus Christ in our weekly services not only devalues him but is also a disservice to worshippers who come to church seeking to know him. The Apostle Paul was certainly capable of speaking on a variety of religious subjects but he explained to his converts: "I determined not to know any thing among you, save Jesus Christ, and him crucified" (1 Cor. 2:2). In many sacrament meetings, I have noticed the tendency to simply mention Jesus' name and then talk about other matters rather than to discuss him and his ministry. In adult Sunday School we teach the Gospels for several months once every four years, then move on to the epistles. In priesthood and Relief Society, the adults study the life and teachings of modern prophets twice a month each year and general conference talks for at least another week each month. We center our discussions on twenty-four gospel topics as identified in the supplementary manuals. Few of these lessons are directly related to Jesus Christ.[3] Active LDS adults can usually recite an overview of Joseph Smith's ministry beginning in New York, then in Ohio, Missouri, Illinois, and his death in 1844 but find it difficult to give an overview of the Savior's three-year ministry beginning in Galilee, the Gentile area, Judea, Peraea, and concluding with Holy Week. (See Appendix.) I would invite the Saints to ask themselves how central Christ's life and ministry are in their study and worship.

These observations have concerned me for a number of years but were amplified several years prior to my assignment at the jail. I was struggling with some of the LDS Church's foundational claims when one night I had a dream that both reflected my difficulties with the Mormon past and offered a clear way of resolving them. I was walking down the street of a suburban neighborhood. The farther I traveled, the darker it became. Turning a street corner, I found myself in total darkness. I searched in vain to find my way, then became frightened and cried out, "How do I find my way"? Behind me I could see a brilliant light. Turning around, I saw the most loving radiant face and person with outstretched arms, seeking to embrace me. It was the Lord Jesus Christ and he said to me: "I am the way."

I awoke from the dream, arose, took my Bible, and read the full verse: "I am the way, the truth, and the life: no man cometh unto the Father, but by me" (John 14:6). I pondered how often Jesus used similar expressions when speaking with his disciples. Jesus asked repeatedly that we focus our attention directly on him: "I am the living bread," "I am the light of the world," "I am the good shepherd," "I am the Son of God," "I am the true vine," "I am the resurrection, and the life," and "I am the door" (John 6:51; 8:12, 10:9, 14, 36; 11:25; 15:1).

Instructing his disciples in desirable behavior, he focused them on him: "Come unto me," "learn of me," "continue with me," "draw nigh unto me," "come after me," "watch with me," "hearken unto me," "look unto me," "follow me," "hear me," "confess me," "gather with me," "remember me," "seek me," "believe on me," "find me," "live by me," "know me," "serve me," "see me," "receive me," "love me," "dwell in me," "honour me," "abide in me," "ask me," "testify of me," and "be witnesses unto me" (Matt. 11:28–29; 15:8, 32; 16:24; 26:38; Mark 7:14; Luke 7:20, 22; 10:16; 11:23; 12:8; 22:19; John 6:26, 47, 56–57; 7:34; 8:19, 54; 12:26, 45; 13:20; 14:23; 15:4, 26; 16:5; Acts 1:8; some verb forms adapted). Jesus uses the phrase "follow me" more than fifteen times when speaking to different individuals and groups in the four Gospels.

The peace and joy this experience brought me created within me the desire to focus more directly on Jesus Christ himself in my church participation. In sacrament meeting, when asked to pray, preach, sing, or testify, I emphasize Christ. The prayers of blessing on the emblems of Christ's life and sacrifice specifically place us under covenant to "remember him." When teaching classes, I make Christ the central figure of whatever scripture, lesson, or course of study is being used. I recommend this course of action to others. Examples from the life of Jesus on faith, love, and forgiveness deepen and enhance the spirituality of our meetings.

Think of the quality of interactions that will occur both at church and at home when a teacher incorporates examples of how Jesus resisted temptation, settled disputes, improved relationships, what he asked for in his prayers, why he returned good for evil, and his way of doing service.

ೞറെ

Notes

1. Retrieved in September 2002 from http://www.adherents.com/Religions_By_Adherents.html; http://www.religioustolerance.org/islam.htm.

2. Arthur R. Bassett, "Knowing, Doing, and Being: Vital Dimensions in the Mormon Religious Experience," *Sunstone* 22 (June 1999): 71; emphasis his.

3. The priesthood/Relief Society manuals used in the LDS Church from 1998 through 2005 contain 192 lessons from the

teachings of Brigham Young, John Taylor, Joseph F. Smith, Heber J. Grant, David O. McKay, and Harold B. Lee. Of these, about twenty are directly related to Jesus Christ.

Chapter 2

Jesus Defines the Christian

To each generation Jesus Christ answers the ancient query of the rich young ruler, "What shall I do to inherit eternal life?" with the timeless response: "Come follow me" (Luke 18:18, 22). The Sermon on the Mount reveals the essential character of Jesus. He defines the Christian to "his disciples" as one who, like himself, practices the beatitudes. Such are promised eternal life in the kingdom of heaven.

Blessed are the poor in spirit: ["disciples" who continue serving diligently when discouraged in bringing others to Christ] for theirs is the kingdom of heaven.

Blessed are they that mourn: for they shall be comforted [in the kingdom of heaven where there is no mourning, pain, or death].

Blessed are the meek: [humble, gentle, long-suffering, not easily offended, self-controlled] for they shall inherit the [new] earth [which will be the kingdom of heaven].

Blessed are they which do hunger and thirst after righteousness: for they shall be filled [with the Spirit, the love of God, wisdom and knowledge in the kingdom of heaven].

Blessed are the merciful: [who are more forgiving than justice requires] for they shall obtain mercy [in the kingdom of heaven].

Blessed are the pure [honest] in heart: for they shall see God [daily, in the kingdom of heaven].

Blessed are the peacemakers: for they shall be called the children [sons and daughters] of God [and inherit all things, in the kingdom of heaven].

Blessed are they which are persecuted for righteousness sake: [return good for evil when reviled, persecuted, or spoken against falsely] for theirs is the kingdom of heaven.

Blessed are ye, when men shall revile you, and persecute you, and shall say all manner of evil against you falsely, for my sake . . . for great is your reward in heaven. (Matt. 5:3-12)

Jesus' life and teaching exemplifies each of these Christian attitude-ideals many times throughout his ministry.

Jesus Is Meek

The Apostles Paul and James refer to "the meekness and gentleness of Christ" (2 Cor. 10:1) and say that his "conversation [and] his works [were appropriately done] with meekness of wisdom" (James 3:13). Jesus himself said: "Learn of me; for I am meek" (Matt. 11:29). For example, in whatever house he entered, he ate the food that was set before him. When a village rejected him, the disciples wanted him to order it consumed by fire, but Jesus rebuked them for their aggressiveness (Luke 10:8; 9:52-56). He made his final entry into Jerusalem "meek, and sitting upon an ass," a symbol of humility for the entry of a king (Matt. 21:5). Jesus was meek (humble, gentle, long suffering, not easily offended, and self-controlled) during his ordeal in Gethsemane, during Judas's betrayal of him, and during his arrest. He showed the "meekness of wisdom" (James 3:13) when controlling his tongue and emotions in court before Annas and Pilate. Before the high priest Caiaphas, "two false witnesses"

Jesus is the Sermon on the Mount

spoke against him, "but Jesus held his peace." Accused by Herod, Jesus "answered him nothing." He continued to show strength under control even when spat on, cursed, scourged, crowned with thorns, and crucified (John 18:19–24, 33–38; Matt. 26:60, 63; Luke 23:8–10; John 19; see cover).

The Old Testament law required that one not kill or commit adultery, but Jesus raised this standard for Christians in his Sermon on the Mount. He expects us to control our anger and lust, the two primary reasons for murder and adultery. Jesus defined sexual lust, not as a thought that passes through the mind, but rather as one that sinks down into the heart. King David is an example. David did not commit adultery "in his heart" when he saw Bathsheba bathing on the roof top, but rather when he yielded to lust, brought her to his house, and gave his lust full reign. Inappropriate thoughts do enter our minds, but we don't have to invite them to dinner. Lust or evil occurs when we take action by planning, plotting, hoping, and creating a scenario for sexual sin to occur. Since Jesus "was in all points tempted like as we are," he undoubtedly experienced sexual temptation (Heb. 4:15). His sermon suggests how he himself handled unsolicited sexual thoughts. He invites us to exercise self discipline, to "pluck it out" or "cut it off"—to remove ourselves from such situations and temptations rather than to "be cast into hell" (Matt. 5:21–30).

Jesus Hungers and Thirsts after Righteousness

Jesus courageously acted from heartfelt conviction when he cleared the merchandisers from the temple courtyard. He did it as a matter of conscience, because it was the right thing to do. He also showed constraint and self-discipline by taking the time to make a whip and by not harming the animals (John 2:14–16).

This strength of character to choose the right is seen throughout Jesus' life. For example, the identifying characteristic of his youth and young adult years is that he "grew, and waxed strong in spirit, filled with wisdom: and the grace of God was upon him" (Luke 2:40). By age thirty, he revealed these spiritual qualities in defeating the adversary. After his baptism, he retreated into the wilderness to fast and meditate upon his imminent ministry. Tempted by the devil, Jesus resisted by being "full of the Holy Ghost." His life was such that he had a full measure of the Spirit. He resisted small temptations such as turning a stone into bread to satisfy his hunger. This would have been a minor miracle for Jesus to perform, but he refused to do so.

Jesus showed his mastery of the scriptures when he answered the devil's temptation all three times by spontaneously quoting from the Old Testament (Deut. 8:3; 6:13–14, 10:20; Exod. 20:3; Deut. 6:16; cf. Luke 4:4, 8, 12). He also knew that he was God's son. When Satan sought to make him doubt this by saying, "If thou be the Son of God. . . ." Jesus responded, "Thou shalt not tempt the Lord thy God." He also placed God above "mammon" (i.e., pursuing the false god of riches and avarice), when Satan tempted him to conquer the cities of the world. He certainly could have become an Alexander the Great and obtained power and wealth. Jesus, however, resisted these three shortcuts and chose instead a spiritual mission that took him to the cross and to the resurrection (Matt. 6:24; Luke 4:1–13).

In other words, Jesus (1) resisted the appeal to appetite, (2) resisted the appeal to pride and honor, and (3) resisted the appeal to power and influence. His thirty-year preparation had brought him to "know" the Father, and "the Father knoweth me" (John 8:55; 10:15). To bring others to know God was clearly his priority. In delivering his important bread of life sermon, Jesus challenged his audience not to be satisfied with a small life, a little daily bread, but to partake of the great spiritual feast that God offers (John 6:22–35).

Thus, when a person seeks the Spirit in his or her life, resists small temptations, knows the scriptures, is confident he or she is a son or daughter of God, and places his or her spiritual life ahead of material things, there is strong assurance that he or she will probably defeat the temptations of the adversary.

Jesus summarized his own life and teaching on the use of time and riches in his sermon by saying: "Seek ye *first* the kingdom of God, and his righteousness; and all these things shall be added unto you" (Matt. 6:33; emphasis mine). Unspoken but strongly implied is: "if you desire them." He urges us to follow the priority of using our time and treasure to help ourselves and others, receiving in return "treasures in heaven," and not worrying overmuch about our worldly goods and financial portfolios (Matt. 6:19–34). He also defines the person who hungers and thirsts after righteousness as one who meditates and prays to God with the faith that he or she will receive answers (Matt. 7:7–11).

Jesus Is More Merciful than Justice Requires

In the story of the woman caught in the act of adultery, Jesus placed her spiritual needs above the Law of Moses and forgave her. It is clear that he did not wish to punish her (John 8:1–11). He seemed to think that the woman's public shame and humiliation were punishment enough. He simply said: "Go, and sin no more."

The parable of the two sons is also an invitation to be more forgiving of others than justice requires. Jesus observed that the Pharisees would neither be seen with nor eat with sinners and thus invited his listeners to be less exclusive and more inclusive in their relationships with sinners. When the younger of the two sons returned home, after abandoning his prodigal ways, the father eagerly ran to welcome him back, not as a servant but as a son—with open arms. The older son, who is a Pharisee, would not attend the feast. Neither would he eat with nor forgive his younger brother. He did not refer to his younger sibling as a brother but as "thy son," i.e., his father's son. In many ways, the elder brother was a model son when relating to all the rules and regulations, the mechanics and customs; but in his failure to show mercy and forgiveness, he sullied his character. The story ends with the father inviting the Pharisee son for a second time to attend the feast and forgive his brother (Luke 15:11-32).

Jesus left the story unfinished, silently inviting his listeners to ponder where they would position themselves on this issue; but the point is clear. Jesus expects us to be more merciful to others than justice requires. He asks that we guide our lives by using the following model. For small misdeeds committed against us, even "seventy times seven" of them, we are to ignore and overlook them (Matt. 18:21-22). If we are unable to heal ourselves of an offense, then we are to go to the offending person alone, and work things out. If this method fails, we are to bring in a third party. Only if this measure also fails should we take the matter to the appropriate authorities (Matt. 18:15-18). By using this process, we will have better relationships and experience life "more abundantly" (John 10:10). In return, God will overlook some of our problems at the judgment.

Jesus reinforced this last point in the parable of the unmerciful servant. In the parable, a servant owed his king an enormous amount of money. Unable to pay, he begged the king to "have patience . . . and I will pay thee all." Moved "with compassion," the king "forgave him the debt." This servant then went out, found a fellow servant who owed him a very small sum of money, and demanded payment in full. Unable to pay, he too begged for mercy. Instead the first servant had him imprisoned. When the king heard of his servant's conduct, he chastised him:

O thou wicked servant, I forgave thee all that debt, because thou desiredst me: Shouldest not thou also have had compassion on thy fellowservant, even as I had pity on thee?

And his lord [king] was wroth, and delivered him to the tormentors, till he should pay all that was due unto him.

So likewise [concluded Jesus] shall my heavenly Father do also unto you, if ye from your hearts forgive not every one his brother their trespasses. (Matt. 18:23-35)

Jesus summarized his own life and teaching on this matter in his Sermon on the Mount, by saying: "If ye forgive men their trespasses, your heavenly Father will also forgive you. But if ye forgive not men their trespasses, neither will your Father forgive your trespasses." Therefore, he concludes epigrammatically, "Judge not, that ye be not judged. For with what judgment ye judge, ye shall be judged: and with what measure ye mete, it shall be measured to you again" (Matt. 6:14-15; 7:1-5).

Jesus Is Pure in Heart

Jesus teaches us what it means to be pure in heart and honest. During his mortal ministry, he spoke his true convictions but was often reviled because of them by religious leaders. His neighbors and relatives also rejected him for telling them forthrightly who he was (Luke 4:16-30; Matt. 13:54-57).

Jesus' true motivations for his actions are seen unequivocally throughout his ministry. For example, two miracles chronicled in the Gospel of John revealed his unassuming and pure nature. The first occurred at a crowded sheep market in Jerusalem. By a pool lay an invalid of thirty-eight years. As Jesus passed by, he paused to talk briefly with the man. Hearing the story of his decades of misery, Jesus was stirred with compassion and commanded: "Rise, take up thy bed, and walk. And immediately the man was made whole . . . and he that was healed wist not who it was: for Jesus had conveyed himself away, a multitude being in that place" (John 5:8-9, 13).

How significant that Jesus quickly healed this man, then left without even waiting to see the success of his action, share the man's joy, and (most tellingly) receive praise for his actions. The healed man didn't even know who had restored him! This incident shows that Jesus was not interested in credit, attention, or fanfare. It reveals the Lord's modest self-effacing nature and demonstrates his true servant-leadership. He simply volunteered to help the man, being sensitive to his need. Nor has his ministry changed today. He still asks, in essence, "How can I help you?" An honest response on our part will meet the same supernal compassion on his.

The second miracle also occurred in Jerusalem, during the Jewish holiday called "the feast of tabernacles." The scribes and pharisees were on the temple grounds, complaining and debating about Jesus and his identity. Jesus joined them and answered candidly: "I am the light of the world: he that followeth me shall not walk in darkness, but shall have the light of life." Their response showed their utter lack of faith: They denied his words and tried to stone him (John 7, 8, esp. 8:12, 59).

Jesus left the temple precinct and immediately encountered "a man which was blind from his birth." Modestly and without fanfare, Jesus then demonstrated that he was literally "the light of the world" by giving the man his sight—enabling him to perceive physical light—but he would not perform this miracle in the presence of unbelievers (John 9:1–7, 12).

There is no indication that Jesus healed either of these men because of their faith. He was simply doing a good deed for two needy people out of his own overflowing goodness. He was following his own teaching of "when thou doest alms [giving time, talents, money], let not thy left hand know what thy right hand doeth." Rather, do good "in secret" (Matt. 6:3–4).

Jesus also teaches us to recognize pure-hearted behavior in the parable of the Good Samaritan. The story is about a

Jesus' way of doing charity

priest, a Levite, a Samaritan, and a man whose race, creed, and color are deliberately unmentioned. This victim had been robbed, beaten, and left to die. The priest and Levite quickly passed on, not offering any aid. In contrast, the Samaritan not only cared for the man, overcoming his own natural fear at the possibility that the robbers would return and attack him, but went the second mile by paying for his care at an inn.

This parable is rich in implications about what constitutes true purity. The Levite and priest ignored the injured man, possibly out of physical fear or, even more likely, to preserve their ritual purity. A strong part of the Mosaic law as practiced at Jesus' time was the numerous rules governing ritual purity (the equivalent to many of our own cultural rules today). Under Levitical law, if these Jews touched a corpse (and perhaps they could not tell if the man was alive or dead), they would be impure or unclean until sundown and hence unable to function in their official capacity. The situation is even more complex when it comes to the victim. According to Jewish law, since Samaritans did not observe laws of ritual purity, the wounded man, if he was a Jew, would have been contaminated by the Samaritan's touch. For him, the situation was literally one of ritual purity (and death) or ritual contamination (and life). Jesus stood this law of ritual purity on its head by pointing out that we are impure in our hearts when we fail to help those in need (Luke 10:30-37).

Jesus also expects us to be honest with ourselves. He detests hypocrisy and asks Christians in the Sermon on the Mount to be pure in motive when giving alms, fasting, and offering public prayers. He warns his disciples:

> Take heed that ye do not your alms [also fasting and prayer] before men, to be seen of them: otherwise ye have no reward of your Father which is in heaven.

> Therefore when thou doest thine alms [and fasting and prayer], do not sound a trumpet before thee [or offer prayers with "much speaking," nor put on "a sad countenance" and act hungry when fasting], as the hypocrites do in the synagogues and in the streets, that they may have glory of men. Verily I say unto you, They have their reward.
>
> But when thou doest alms [also fasting and prayer], let not thy left hand know what thy right hand doeth . . . [do alms] in secret: and thy Father which seeth in secret himself shall reward thee openly. (Matt. 6:1-4; cf. 6:5-13, 16-18)

Jesus is honest in presenting this choice. The test is about motive, about choosing a blessing from God or receiving the praise of men. We cannot have it both ways. He also asks us in this sermon to simply tell the truth. He teaches that answering yes or no is sufficient. Swearing to oaths by heaven and earth, by temple ritual, upon your mother's grave, or in any other way dictated by culture and custom are unnecessary (Matt. 5:33-37; cf. James 5:12).

Jesus Is a Peacemaker

As the Prince of Peace, Jesus not only demonstrates his lack of prejudice but also teaches us how to overcome it. He revealed this quality by asking a Samaritan woman at Jacob's well for a drink of water. She was shocked that a Jew would even speak to a Samaritan, let alone request water from her. Jesus responded with what amounts to a request that she make a request of him: saying in effect, If you will ask me, I will give you a drink and more. Jesus treated her more kindly and respectfully than she expected and consequently made friends of the entire town (John 4:5-10, 40).

Jesus used this same principle on a rich man named Zacchaeus, who "was the chief among the publicans." As a tax collector over the entire district, he was universally despised. Yet in front of a large crowd, Jesus announced that he intended

Jesus treating a Samaritan more respectfully than she expects

to become Zacchaeus's guest. He treated Zacchaeus far better than the little tax collector was accustomed to being treated. As a result, Zacchaeus became a Christian and gave half of his goods to the poor (Luke 19:1–10).

This principle—of being a peacemaker, approaching others with kindness and respect—is a model for obtaining peace in our troubled relationships, whether personal or business.

In the Sermon on the Mount, Jesus also asks: "If any man will sue thee at the law, and [wants to] take away thy coat, [offer, or] let him have thy cloke also" (Matt. 5:40). The message in our litigious times is clear: Spread the message of the Prince of Peace by seeking to settle your differences out of court. Make your offer better than your opponent anticipates it to be.

Jesus further instructs us that when someone in authority over us "shall compel thee to go a mile, go with him twain" (Matt. 5:41), i.e., carry out the assignment, then do more than is required. Moreover, "Give to him that asketh thee, and from him that would borrow of thee turn not thou away" (Matt. 5:42). Thus, when a beggar asks, give him something, for he usually receives little or nothing. However, in many cities today, free meals and shelter are provided by city officials. They usually request that money not be given in order to discourage begging. If a person desires to borrow from us, try to be generous in the terms, keeping in mind that the best form of lending money is probably that which helps people to help themselves.

Jesus Returns Good for Evil

When Jesus was reviled, persecuted, and falsely accused by others, he turned the other cheek, returning good for evil. He continued to invite his persecutors to the great feast, the abundant life. Only at the very end of his life did he condemn some of the religious leaders for their absolute hypocrisy and self-righteousness (Matt. 23). Jesus often received maltreatment and serious persecution from the Jewish leadership and others.

They repeatedly bore "false witness against Jesus," calling him a "deceiver" and "accused him of many things." They "reviled him," for associating with "sinners," and accused him of being "a gluttonous man, and a winebibber." "They derided him," "laughed him to scorn" and "rejected him." They continually said that he was born out of wedlock, "born of fornication," "born in sin." They called him "a Samaritan" "a sinner," and possessed of the "devil." While he was in jail, his guards "stripped him, and put on him a scarlet robe . . . a crown of thorns, . . . and a reed [staff] in his right hand: And they bowed the knee before him, and mocked him . . . they spit upon him . . . and smote him on the head." They "scourged him," made him "bear his cross," and "crucified him." And "they that passed by [his cross] railed on him, wagging their heads" (Matt. 26:59; 27:26–32, 39, 63; Mark 5:40; 15:3, 29, 32; Luke 5:30; 7:34; 16:14; 17:25; John 8:41, 48; 9:24, 28, 34; 10:20).

Jesus' own family "were offended at him" neither "did his brethren [siblings] believe in him." The Apostles Paul and Peter said, speaking of all these false accusations, revilements, and persecutions, that Jesus simply "endured the . . . shame," for "when he was reviled, [he] reviled not; when he suffered, he threatened not" (Mark 6:1–3; John 7:5; Heb. 12:2; 1 Pet. 2:23). He continued to socialize and eat with sinners and the poor even though he was despised for his openness. He did his "mighty works" even when his life was threatened (Matt. 11:20; Mark 6:2; 11:18).

When Jesus told his disciples that his soul was "troubled" about his forthcoming atoning sacrifice, he ended up comforting *them*. He faced that terrible ordeal knowing that all of his disciples would shortly forsake and/or betray him, including Judas, and yet he prayed for them and washed their feet. When he was arrested, he made certain that his disciples escaped. When Peter bravely but foolishly tried to defend him and sliced off Malchus's ear, Jesus replaced and healed it.

When most people are wounded and suffering, they usually turn inward and feel sorry for themselves. Jesus turned outward and thought of others, even on the cross. He forgave the Roman guards who crucified him, spoke comforting words to the thief next to him who had previously "reviled him," and asked John to care for his mother. To the other apostles who forsook him and "stood afar off" during the crucifixion, his first words to them three days later were, "Peace be unto you" (Mark 15:32; John 12–19; Luke 23:49; 24:36).

Jesus predicated his own life and teaching on this point in the Sermon on the Mount by saying: "Love your enemies, bless them that curse you, do good to them that hate you, and pray for them which despitefully use you, and persecute you" (Matt. 5:44). Jesus truly "suffered many things" but was "made perfect" by this teaching, as was Peter (Mark 9:12; Heb. 5:8–9). After a lifetime of experience, Peter knowingly promised the Saints who returned good for evil that "Christ Jesus, after that ye have suffered a while, [will] make you perfect" by his "strengthen[ing]" grace (1 Pet. 5:10; for other promises see 1 Pet. 2:12, 15, 3:16; 3:9, 12; 4:16–19).

Jesus cautioned his followers against behaving in a way that brought reviling and persecution upon themselves unnecessarily. He said: "Give not that which is holy unto the dogs, neither cast ye your pearls before swine, lest they trample them under their feet, and turn again and rend you." The Apostle Paul made this mistake when he shared with a hostile crowd of unbelievers his Christian conversion story on the road to Damascus. The crowd, rather than being touched, sought to kill him (Matt. 5:43–48; 7:6; Acts 21–22).

In short, in the beatitudes, Jesus defines the Christian as a person who:

- Is diligent in the ministry.
- Exercises self-discipline.
- Does what is right.

- Forgives others beyond what justice requires.
- Is pure in heart and honest.
- Is a peacemaker.
- Returns good for evil.

He asked that we internalize these attitudes: "For . . . except your righteousness shall exceed the righteousness of the scribes and Pharisees, ye shall in no case enter into the kingdom of heaven" (Matt. 5:20).

In this sermon, Jesus explains that, when these Christian attitudes are in us, becoming part of our very nature, we are "the salt of the earth," "the light of the world," "a city that is set on a hill [and that] cannot be hid." He promises that we will radiate "the light," for "your light [will] so shine before men" (Matt. 5:13–16).

David O. McKay, the ninth President of the Church of Jesus Christ of Latter-day Saints, amplified and clarified this teaching:

> It was the divine character of Jesus that drew the women of Palestine to him, that drew as a magnet the little children to him. It was that divine personality which attracted men, honest men, [and] pure men. It was also that divine personality which antagonized the impure, the evil men and women. . . . It is the radiation of the light that attracts. . . . When the people came to Jesus and asked for bread, or the truth, he never turned them away with a stone. He always had truth to give. He understood it. It radiated from his being. . . .
>
> Every man and every person who lives in this world wields an influence, whether for good or for evil. It is not what he says alone, it is not alone what he does. It is what he is. Every man, every person radiates what he or she is. Every person is a recipient of radiation. The Savior was conscious of that. Whenever he came into the presence of an individ-

ual, he sensed that radiation—whether it was the woman of
Samaria with her past life; whether it was the woman who
was to be stoned or the men who were to stone her; whether
it was the statesman, Nicodemus, or one of the lepers. He was
conscious of the radiation from the individual. And to a
degree so are you, and so am I. It is what we are and what we
radiate that affects the people around us . . . If we think noble
thoughts, if we encourage and cherish noble aspirations,
there will be that radiation when we meet people, especially
when we associate with them. . . . The Savior set us the example, always calm, always controlled, radiating something
which people could feel as they passed—the woman who
touched his garment. He felt something go from him, that
radiation which is divine. Each individual soul has it. This is
you. The body is only the house in which you live. God help
us to radiate strength, control, love, charity, which is another name for love, consideration, [and] best wishes for all
human beings. . . .

There is one responsibility that no man can evade. That
is the responsibility of personal influence. The effect of your
words and acts is tremendous in this world. Every moment of
life you are changing to a degree the life of the whole world.
Every man has an atmosphere or a radiation that is affecting
every person in the world. You cannot escape it. Into the
hands of every individual is given a marvelous power for
good or for evil. It is simply the constant radiation of what a
man really is. Every man by his mere living is radiating posi-
tive or negative qualities. Life is a state of radiation. To exist
is to be the radiation of our feelings, natures, doubts,
schemes, or to be the recipient of those things from some-
body else. You cannot escape it. Man cannot escape for one
moment the radiation of his character. You will select the
qualities that you will permit to be radiated.[1]

Jesus completed his Sermon on the Mount in Matthew
7:13–29 by observing that following him is not like driving on
an easy boulevard, but rather like making our way on a strait

and narrow path which leads to a small gate. "I am the door" he said. "By me if any man shall enter in, he shall be saved." True prophets teach, focus on, and practice these sayings (John 10:9); and "Whosoever shall do and teach them, the same shall be called great in the kingdom of heaven" (Matt. 5:19). "False prophets," Jesus explains, may have "prophesied, . . . cast out devils" and "done many wonderful works" in my name, "but he that doeth [not] the will of my Father . . . will I profess unto them [at the door], I never knew you: depart from me, ye that work iniquity" (Matt. 7:15, 21–23). Jesus concludes:

> Therefore whosoever heareth these sayings of mine, and doeth them, I will liken him unto a wise man, which built his house upon a rock. And the rain descended, and the floods came, and the winds blew, and beat upon that house; and it fell not: for it was founded upon a rock. And every one that heareth these sayings of mine, and doeth them not, shall be likened unto a foolish man, which built his house upon the sand. And the rain descended, and the floods came, and the winds blew, and beat upon that house; and it fell: and great was the fall of it. (Matt. 7:24–27)

To assist us in taking upon ourselves the divine nature, Jesus Christ asks that we enter into a covenant with God. In the first LDS sacramental prayer, the blessing on the bread, we are to ask ourselves anew each week if we "are *willing* to take upon us the name of God's Son, and always remember *him* [his character] and keep his commandments . . . that we may always have his Spirit to be with us" (D&C 20:77; paraphrased, emphasis mine). Remembering him brings the promise of his Spirit to be with us, which prepares us for the events and challenges of the coming week. Such a lifetime commitment brings unity with him and the abundant life he promises: "I am with you alway[s]." "My peace I give unto you." "[My Spirit] shall teach you all things . . . whatsoever I have said." And "I will love you, and will manifest myself to you," a fullness of which is realized in "the kingdom of heaven" (Matt. 28:20; John 14:26-27; John 14:21, paraphrased; Rev. 21-22).

It is my lifetime observation, which includes counseling thousands of inmates at the Salt Lake County Jail for many years, that those who fail to "remember him"—those who are the furthest away from living these Christian ideals—are having the most difficult lives. People who fail to follow the way of the Prince of Peace, the Good Shepherd, the Light of the World, the True Vine, the Bread of Life, and the Living Water are troubled and lost, wandering in the dark, despairing, hungry and thirsty.

ഇ൭ൠ

Note

1. David O. McKay, "Spirituality in Leading and Teaching the Gospel," *Improvement Era* 71 (December 1968): 108-9; "Radiation of the Gospel," ibid., 66 (June 1963): 533-35; "To Be in the Service of Our Fellowmen Is to Be in the Service of Our God," ibid., 72 (Dec. 1969): 87.

Chapter 3

The Kingdom of Heaven

The rewards for living the beatitudes include receiving eternal life with God and Christ in the kingdom of heaven, a compensation that is often overlooked. This chapter focuses on describing this kingdom, including the specific blessings Jesus promises in the beatitude portion of his Sermon on the Mount. Jesus begins and closes his beatitudes by affirming to his disciples that, when serving God and becoming "poor in spirit," "reviled" or "persecuted for righteousness sake" their reward "is the kingdom of heaven" (Matt. 5:3, 10).

We find the finest image of this promised kingdom, whether one views it as a literal description or as allegory, in the last two chapters of the book of Revelation (Rev. 21–22). Jesus instructed his angel to describe the holy city to John as follows. Like the Holy of Holies in Solomon's temple, the shape of the eternal city is as long as it is wide and as high as it is long (1 Kgs. 6:19–20). In other words it is laid out like a vast cube. Each dimension is equally "twelve thousand furlongs" (ca. 1,500 miles). The length of the new Zion would be approximately from Salt Lake City, Utah, to Cleveland, Ohio. The width roughly corresponds to the width of the United States running from Canada to Mexico. The celestial city is also 1,500 miles high and may be three-tiered. In this respect the Apostle Paul said that he had visited "the third heaven" [tier] of this king-

33

dom, and reported that "eye hath not seen, nor ear heard, neither have entered into the heart of [mortal] man, the things which God hath prepared for them that love him" (2 Cor. 12:2-4; 1 Cor. 2:9).

The squared city is walled and has twelve gates, each gate being made of a large pearl. There are three gates each on the east, north, south, and west walls. They are always open, but an angel is assigned to guard each gate. The wall is "high," 144 cubits thick (ca. 216 ft.) and is made of jasper, with eleven other precious stones used in layers for decorative purposes. The twelve stones used are: jasper, sapphire, chalcedony (agate), emerald, sardonyx (onyx), sardius (ruby), chrysolite, beryl, topaz, chrysoprasus, jacinth, and amethyst. In the Old Testament, these stones, with three exceptions, were located in the high priest's breastplate and are associated with the Urim and Thummim (cf. Exod. 28:17-21; 39:10-14 with Rev. 21:19-20). If allowance is made for the differences between the Hebrew and Greek names, the stones may in fact be the same. Thus, the breastplate seemingly served as a dim representation or symbol of the heavenly city. The streets of the city appear to be made of pure gold, like transparent glass. The golden city requires no sun, moon, or lamp as the glory from the Father and the Son and the other kingly (and possibly queenly) inhabitants provide the light. There is never any darkness. The precious stones of the walls and streets reflecting the glory of these beings would indeed create a bright and shiny "city that is set on a hill [and] cannot be hid" (Rev. 21:10-27; cf. Matt. 5:14).

Jesus also promised in the beatitudes, "Blessed are the meek: for they shall inherit the earth" (i.e., live in the eternal city on the new earth). John said that he was carried away "in the spirit to a great and high mountain" (Rev. 21:10). Here he stated that, at the close of the millennial era:

I saw a new heaven and a new earth . . . and there was no more sea.

And I John [also] saw the holy city, new Jerusalem, coming down from God out of heaven . . .

Behold, the tabernacle of God is with men, and he will dwell with them, and they shall be his people. (Rev. 21:1-3; cf. 2 Pet. 3:13)

Jesus added, "[I will] receive you unto myself; that where I am, there ye may be also." In the "many mansions" of the celestial city, God and man will dwell together (John 14:2-3).

Jesus also affirmed in the beatitudes, "Blessed are they that mourn: for they shall be comforted." John saw the fulfillment of this promise in the eternal city:

God shall wipe away all tears from their eyes; and there shall be no more death, neither sorrow, nor crying, neither shall there be any more pain: for the former things are passed away.

And he that sat upon the throne said, Behold, I make all things new. (Rev. 21:4-5)

Jesus further pledged in the beatitudes, "Blessed are they which do hunger and thirst after righteousness: for they shall be filled" (with the love of God, wisdom, and knowledge in the heavenly city). Recall that Adam and Eve in the Garden of Eden were denied access to "the tree of life" by an angel because they had not yet received the necessary experience "to know good and evil" in mortality. John, however, saw that the inhabitants of the holy city who had overcome the world, "have right to the tree of life, and may enter in through the gates [past the sentinel] into the city" and "eat of the tree of life" (Gen. 3:22-24; Rev. 22:14; 2:7).

Jesus also continued: "I will give unto him that is athirst of the fountain of the water of life freely." The river of life and the tree of life are located "in the midst of the paradise [city] of God" (Rev. 21:6, 2:7). The river flows from the throne of God and the Lamb, sustaining the tree of life. John actually described trees of life on both sides of the river. The trees bear twelve kinds of fruit or food, probably in succession rather than at the same time, one each month. The trees and their leaves are "for the healing of the nations" (Rev. 22:1–2; cf. Ezek. 47:12).

Also represented by the tree of life is the love of God, which fills the city and is undoubtedly responsible for this "healing." The fruit of the tree and the river of water may be for nourishment to those dwelling in the city of God, but John saw that the citizens also received another kind of nourishment. He reported that the inhabitants would "eat of the hidden manna, and [I] will give him a white stone, and in the stone a new name written, which no man knoweth saving he that receiveth it" (Rev. 2:17; cf. D&C 130:10–11). This computer-like device is activated by a specific name or password, which provides real online access to the vast knowledge and wisdom of the cosmos, the "hidden manna" as it were. Rather than a worldwide web, a universe-wide web becomes accessible.

Jesus also declared in the beatitudes, "Blessed are the merciful [i.e., those who show more mercy to others than they deserve]: for they shall obtain mercy." In a special ceremony before God in the hall of heroes, Jesus promised in his mercy that each person

> shall be clothed in white raiment; and I will not blot out his name out of the book of life, but I will confess his name before my Father, and before his angels . . .
>
> And I will write upon him the name of my God, and the name of the city of my God . . .
>
> I will write upon him my new name . . . I [will] grant [him] to sit with me in my throne, even as I also overcame, and am set down with my Father in his throne. (Rev. 3:5, 12, 21)

Jesus also in his mercy promised, "[To] him will I give power over the nations . . . even as I received of my Father. And I will give him the morning star" (which is another title of Jesus Christ). Under Jesus' personal tutelage, instead of receiving only the partial dominion and power bestowed upon humankind in the Garden of Eden, we will receive full dominion, knowledge, and power over the earth (Gen. 1:28; Rev. 2:26–28; 22:16). Christ's willingness to share with us his throne, which represents his glory, power, knowledge, and dominion, is an exceptional act of grace!

Jesus also affirmed in the beatitudes, "Blessed are the pure in heart: for they shall see God." In the city John saw stood "the throne of God and of the Lamb . . . and his servants shall serve him. And they shall see his face," for "God himself shall be with them, and be their God" (Rev. 21:3; 22:3–4). Daily interactions with the Father and the Son are an inestimable blessing.

Jesus finally promised in the beatitudes, "Blessed are the peacemakers: for they shall be called the children of God." In this city, each son and daughter "shall inherit all things; and I will be his God, and he shall be my son" (Rev. 21:7). Being a "son" makes him an heir, for a servant does not "inherit all things." Moreover, Jesus "hath made us kings and priests unto God and his Father." With such an important inheritance at stake, God cautions us in this life to "hold that fast which thou hast, that no man take[s] thy crown" (Rev. 1:6; 3:11). The presence of kings in the heavenly kingdom also suggests queens and hopefully a family relationship. (See D&C 132:19.)

I believe that prior to our earth life, we lived in this very city and that we now hope to return and become rightful heirs as tested sons and daughters of God. Bible references and "The Hymn of the Pearl," an early Christian document, further express such sentiments (Rev. 12:4, 7–9; Jude 1:6; Rom. 8:29;

Eph. 1:4; Acts 17:28–29; Ps. 82:6; D&C 49:17; D&C 93:23, 29). "The Pearl" was discovered at Nag Hammadi, Egypt, in 1945. Many scholars believe it was written during the first or second century A.D. The document is attributed to the Apostle Thomas. While teaching the gospel in a foreign land, Thomas's message of his new-proclaimed God offended the king, who imprisoned him. He prayed, and soon the other prisoners asked him to pray for them. Thomas complied and began to utter a psalm:

> When I was a little child
> And dwelt in my kingdom, the house of my father,
> And enjoyed the wealth and the luxuries
> Of those who brought me up,
> From the East [heaven], our homeland,
> My parents provisioned and sent me. . . .
> And they took off from me the splendid robe
> Which in their love they had wrought for me,
> And the purple toga,
> Which was woven to the measure of my stature,
> And they made with me a covenant
> And wrote it in my heart, that I might not forget:
> > "If thou go down to Egypt [the world]
> > And bring the one pearl [a proven character]
> > Which is in the midst of the sea,
> > In the abode of the loud-breathing serpent,
> > Thou shalt put on (again) thy splendid robe
> > And thy toga which lies over it,
> > And with thy brother, our next in rank,
> > Thou shalt be heir in our kingdom."
> I quitted the East and went down,
> Led by two couriers,
> For the way was dangerous and difficult
> And I was very young to travel it. . . .
> I went down into Egypt,
> And my companions parted from me.

I went straight to the serpent,
Near by his abode I stayed,
Until he should slumber and sleep,
That I might take my pearl from him.
And since I was all alone
I was a stranger to my companions of my hostelry.
But one of my race I saw there,
A nobleman out of the East,
A youth fair and lovable,
An anointed one,
And he came and attached himself to me
And I made him my intimate friend,
My companion to whom I communicated my business.
I (He?) warned him (me?) against the Egyptians
And against consorting with the unclean.
But I clothed myself in garments like theirs,
That they might not suspect that I was come from without
To take the pearl,
And so might waken the serpent against me.
But from some cause or other
They perceived that I was not their countryman,
And they dealt with me treacherously
And gave me to eat of their [forbidden] food.
And I *forgot* that I was a king's son
And served their king.
And I forgot the pearl
For which my parents had sent me.
And because of the heaviness of their food
I fell into a deep sleep.
And all this that befell me
My parents observed and were grieved for me.
And a proclamation was published in our kingdom
That all should come to our gate,
The kings and chieftains of Parthia
And all the great ones of the East.
They made a resolve concerning me,
That I should not be left in Egypt,

And they wrote to me a letter
And every noble set his name thereto:
>   "From thy father, the king of kings,
>   And thy mother, the mistress of the East,
>   And from thy brother, our other son,
>   To thee, our son in Egypt, greeting!
>   Awake and rise up from thy sleep,
>   And hearken to the words of our letter.
>   *Remember* that thou art a son of kings.
>   See the slavery—him whom thou dost serve!
>   *Remember* the pearl
>   For which thou didst journey into Egypt.
>   *Remember* thy splendid robe,
>   And think of thy glorious toga,
>   That thou mayest put them on and deck thyself
>   therewith,
>   That thy name may be read in the book of the
>   heroes
>   And thou with thy brother, our crown prince,
>   Be heir in our kingdom."

And the letter was a letter
Which the king had sealed with his right hand. . . .
It flew in the form of an eagle,
The king of all birds,
It flew and alighted beside me
And became all speech [i.e., became a familiar sound
    inside his head].
At its voice and the sound of its rustling
I awoke and stood up from my sleep,
I took it and kissed it,
Broke its seal and read.
And even as it was engraven in my heart
Were the words of my letter written.
I *remembered* that I was a son of kings
And my noble birth asserted itself.
I *remembered* the pearl

For which I was sent to Egypt,
And I began to cast a spell
On the terrible loud-breathing serpent.
I brought him to slumber and sleep
By naming my father's name over him,
And the name of our next in rank
And of my mother, the queen of the East.
And I snatched away the pearl
And turned about, to go to my father's house.
And their dirty and unclean garment
I took off and left in their land,
And directed my way that I might come
To the light of our homeland, the East. . . .
And my splendid robe which I had taken off,
And my toga with which it was wrapped about,
From the heights of Warkan (Hyrcania)
My parents sent thither
By the hand of their treasurers,
Who for their faithfulness were trusted therewith.
Indeed I remembered no more its dignity,
For I had left it in my childhood in my father's house,
But suddenly, when I saw it over against me,
The splendid robe became like me, as my reflection in a
       mirror . . .
And I stretched out and took it.
With the beauty of its colours I adorned myself.
And my toga of brilliant colours
I drew completely over myself.
I clothed myself with it and mounted up
To the gate of greeting and homage.
I bowed my head and worshiped
The splendor of the father who had sent it (the robe) to
       me,
Whose commands I had accomplished,
As he also had done what he promised.
And at the gate of his satraps
I mingled among his great ones.

For he rejoiced over me and received me,
And I was with him in his kingdom.
And with the sound of the organ
All his servants praise him.
And he promised me that to the gate
Of the king of kings I should journey with him again
And with my gift and my pearl
With him appear before our king.[1]

The purpose of the son's appearing before "the king of kings" with his "pearl" (a proven character) in his "splendid robe," is so "that thy name may be read in the book of the heroes, and thou with thy brother, our crown prince, be heir in our kingdom." These motifs and others similar to it also appear in the book of Revelation (cf. Rev. 1:6; 3:5, 11, 21).

Finally, Jesus promised us a sacramental meal with him in this life and in the kingdom of heaven: "Behold I stand at the door, and knock; If any man hear my voice, and open the door, I will come in to him and sup with him, and he with me." Jesus explicitly told to his disciples: "Ye may eat and drink *at my table in my kingdom*" (Rev. 3:20; Luke 22:30; emphasis mine). My brother Glade received this sacral meal with Jesus at a difficult time of his life. He wrote:

During February 1994, I experienced chronic pain and depression due to thrombi-phlebitis and the loss of my employment. I had a hopeless perspective for my future and wondered how long I would live. Under these circumstances, I asked God in fervent prayer to know the nature of eternal life. During the night I dreamed that I was standing in a street of the heavenly city. . . . All around me, as well as within me there was an immense and over-powering radiation of love. I felt completely healed and comforted by this love which satisfied my every need and desire. In fact this love seemed to be life itself. I felt I could be completely happy here. This love healed my pain and depression and lifted my spirit. Seeking to find its source I was drawn to a nearby house and I knocked at the door. A voice within bid me to enter. Upon entering, I saw standing about six feet away the Lord Jesus Christ. He asked me to sit down at the table near him. The table and chairs were of heavy wood and looked to be hand-made. Jesus, while standing, broke a loaf of bread in half and put half on two plates. He then poured wine into my cup and then into his. He told me to eat and drink and as he did so said, "Let me tell you about eternal life. This love which you now feel is the fullness of my love. Share all the love that is within you and with everyone regardless of who they are or whether they deserve it. Don't expect anything in return from them. Do this and I will fill you with the fullness of my love, which love is eternal life." With these words the dream came to a close.

My brother's dream-experience strikes me as fulfilling the Lord's promise. He supped at the Lord's own table, experiencing a holy communion and union with Jesus Christ himself. It was indeed a sacrament. He received broken bread from the Bread of Life, wine from the Living Water, and heard an explanation of the nature of eternal life by Eternal Life.

In the Sermon on the Mount, we see Jesus both defining the Christian and also see Jesus' essential character revealed. To those practicing the beatitudes—i.e., to the one who "heareth these sayings of mine and doeth them"—Jesus promises the kingdom of heaven (Matt. 7:24). In the book of Revelation, as we have seen, Jesus gives details on each of his beatitude promises: We will live with God and Christ in a beautiful city and interact with them frequently. Sorrow and mourning will be no more. In this city, the love of God abounds and there is access to the wisdom and knowledge of the universe. As his sons and daughters, we will "inherit all things," sharing his throne, wisdom, glory, power and dominion. It is ironical but not surprising that some of the churches today require more of their members to enter the city of God than Jesus!

ഇൻരു

Note

1. "The Pearl," translated by R. McL. Wilson in *New Testament Apocrypha*, edited by Wilhelm Schneemelcher, 2 vols. (Philadelphia: Westminster Press, 1964), 2:15–16, 435, 498–504, emphasis mine, brackets mine, parentheses Wilson's.

Chapter 4

The Character of Jesus

When Philip, one of Jesus' apostles, asks him to "shew us the Father," Jesus replied: "He that hath seen me hath seen the Father . . . [because] I am in the Father, and the Father in me" (John 14:8-10). Jesus Christ is the reflection of God to this world, representing both his character and personality. Because this is true, we ought to read the four Gospels closely, looking for how Jesus and the Father *reveal themselves* to us within the incidents and teachings of Jesus' life. Examples of reading the scriptures using this method follow.

God's Respect for Free Agency

One evening on the shore of the Sea of Galilee, Jesus unexpectedly said:

> Let us pass over unto the other side . . .
> And there arose a great storm of wind, and the waves beat into the ship, so that it was now full . . .
> [Jesus] rebuked the wind, and said unto the sea, Peace, be still. And the wind ceased, and there was a great calm. (Mark 4:35, 37, 39)
> When he was come out of the ship, immediately there met him out of the tombs a man with an unclean spirit,

Who had his dwelling among the tombs: and no man
could bind him, no, not with chains:

Because that he had been often bound with fetters and
chains, and the chains had been plucked asunder by him, and
the fetters broken in pieces: neither could any man tame him.

And always, night and day, he was in the mountains, and
in the tombs, crying, and cutting himself with stones . . .

[Jesus] said unto him, Come out of the man, thou
unclean spirit. (Mark 5:2-6, 8)

After liberating this man, Jesus then "passed over again
by ship unto the other side" of Galilee, where he had first begun
the trip (Mark 5:21). The record does not suggest any other
activities, leaving us to conclude that Jesus made this brief
excursion apparently for the sole purpose of returning this tor-
mented individual's free agency to him.

The Adversary, apparently seeking to deter Jesus, caused
the terrible storm that Jesus quelled, almost effortlessly. This
incident reveals the profound respect that Jesus has—and that
we should have—for a person's right to freely exercise his or her
agency.

Jesus also taught this principle in the parable of the four
soils (Luke 8:5-15), where he clearly shows his respect for each
person's right to freely choose even a matter of such eternal
moment as salvation. Jesus observes, without words of harsh
condemnation or violent scolding, though surely with some sorrow, that some individuals will ignore him altogether by simply
allowing his words to fall "by the way side." Some make an ini-
tial choice of accepting his message but develop "no root; . . .
[thus] in time of temptation," they possess no strength to resist
it and return to their old friends, habits, and ways. The third
group also chooses to accept him but eventually are "choked
with cares and riches and pleasures of this life, and bring no
fruit to perfection." Still others choose with "an honest and

good heart, having heard the word, keep it, and bring forth fruit with patience" (vv. 5, 13-15).

These choices are not necessarily permanent or irreversible. My personal lifelong experience, multiplied many times by observing my students, is that God's influence is often silently but busily at work in our lives, making the soil ready to produce more "fruit." Some people are simply not yet ready, but any soil can be prepared.

Jesus' Acceptance of Others' Love

One week before the Lord died, Mary knew his death was nigh. She took some ointment and "anointed the feet of Jesus, and wiped his feet with her hair: and the house was filled with the odour of the ointment." One of the twelve apostles criticized her for this action because this substance was "very costly," but Jesus responded, "Let her alone: against the day of my burying hath she kept this" (John 12:3, 7).

While the apostles were looking for a liberating Messiah, Mary saw the shadow of the cross. Being sensitive to her insight, Jesus allowed her to make her gift to him, accepting it graciously and validating her warmly. Mary was giving him her very best—as should we. Jesus did not need Mary's gift, but he knew that Mary needed to show him her love. For Jesus, this episode was not about the ointment. It was about Mary. He did not demean her gift; he simply appreciated it. This incident reveals that Jesus not only loves tenderly but allows us to love him and accepts our efforts, even though they are doubtless sometimes awkward, to show it.

We see another example of Jesus accepting a person's love during a dinner party. Simon, a Pharisee, invited some friends to his house. Jesus was among the guests. A woman, who had apparently been affected by Jesus' teaching, came into the house "weeping, and began to wash his feet with tears, and did wipe them with the hairs of her head, and kissed his feet, and anointed them with the ointment" (Luke 7:38). Simon knew her by reputation as a "sinner" (v. 39) whom he believed should be ostracized, especially by someone claiming to be a religious leader. Obviously, her actions embarrassed Simon, who was startled because Jesus did not respond in the same way. Rather, Jesus saw a woman in a tender moment, overcome with gratitude and love for the individual who had brought her to the point where she could embrace a new life. She needed to express those overwhelming feelings, and Jesus graciously accepted her gift—seeing past the extravagance, emotionality, and embarrassment that stopped his host.

Jesus' Empathy for Others

The Gospel of John records the death of Lazarus and how Jesus called him back from the dead (John 11:1–46). Jesus was good friends, not only with Lazarus but also with his sisters, Mary and Martha; he often stayed at their Bethany home when he was visiting Jerusalem. Four days after Lazarus's funeral, Jesus arrived in Bethany where the sorrowful sisters greeted him. When he saw them "weeping . . . Jesus wept" (v. 33, 35). We know why Mary, Martha, and their friends were crying, but why would Jesus weep, knowing full well that within minutes he would raise Lazarus from the dead? I believe that Jesus wept for their sorrow. He bore and shared their burden and loss. Truly, as Savior, Jesus mourns with those who mourn. He also teaches us that adult men with reason to weep should not withhold their tears.

His Intervention in Our Lives

Near the Sea of Galilee, Jesus "departed into a mountain to pray," while his disciples launched their boat on the Galilee:

And when even was come [i.e., during the first watch, 6-9 P.M.], the ship was in the midst of the sea, and he alone on the land.

And he saw them toiling in rowing; for the wind was contrary unto them: and about the fourth watch of the night he cometh unto them [3-6 A.M.], walking upon the sea . . .

And he went up unto them into the ship; and the wind ceased. (Mark 6:46-48, 51)

Jesus left his disciples during the first watch and came to them during the fourth. Thus, they had been "toiling" for nearly twelve hours against the wind, going nowhere. It would not have been unreasonable for them to wish, once they were safe again, that Jesus had intervened during the first watch. But he didn't. Likewise, Jesus may come to us, not in the first, second or third, but during the fourth watch. However, we may have confidence that we have been in his attention all the time, just as he was watching the disciples ("saw them toiling in rowing") from the mountain top. He allows us to grow by wrestling with our challenges, often intervening only after a trial of our faith.

Jesus Teaches Equality under the Law

A brief yet interesting episode in the life of Jesus centers on the temple tax. Under Jewish law, all males age twenty and over were assessed an annual temple tax for maintaining the building itself and for underwriting the worship services. However, kings and their children were exempt.

When the tax collector came to Peter's house, he asked, "Doth not your master pay tribute?" Peter answered yes and went to get the half-shekel tax, but "Jesus prevented him" (Matt. 17:24-25). Paying the tax could be construed by others as Jesus' admission that he was not a king or a king's son. However, Jesus did not believe that kings and their children should be above the law. He resolved this dilemma by paying the tax but in a way that demonstrated both his royalty and his divinity. He instructed Peter: "Go thou to the sea, and cast an hook, and take up the fish that first cometh up; and when thou hast opened his mouth, thou shalt find a piece of money: that take, and give unto them for me and thee" (v. 27).

Jesus' View on the Church and Equality

Jesus took a generous view of individuals and churches that do his work, but which lack his express authority. The newly chosen apostles, who were obviously disturbed about the question of authority, complained to Jesus:

> We saw one casting out devils in thy name, and he followeth not us: and we forbad him, because he followeth not us.
> But Jesus said, Forbid him not: for there is no man which shall do a miracle in my name, that can lightly speak evil of me.
> For he that is not against us is on our part.
> For whosoever shall give you a cup of water to drink in my name, because ye belong to Christ, verily I say unto you, he shall not lose his reward. (Mark 9:38-41; cf. Luke 9:49-50)

Jesus later amplified this teaching, explaining that when he returns in glory at his second coming, he will judge "all nations: and he shall separate them [the people] one from another, as a shepherd divideth his sheep from the goats" (meaning the righteous from the wicked). Importantly, he identified those who will "inherit the kingdom" and receive "life eternal," as those who minister to the "hungr[y] . . . thirsty . . . stranger . . . naked . . . sick . . . [or] in prison," and reiterated: "Inasmuch as ye have done it unto one of the least of these my brethren, ye have done it unto me" (Matt. 25:32, 46, 34-36, 40).

In contrast to this abundant approval and validation is Jesus' disappointment with Church members who have high expectations of entering the city of God but who do not *know* him. Speaking in the context of practicing the beatitudes, Jesus declared:

> Not every one that saith unto me, Lord, Lord, shall enter into the kingdom of heaven; but he that doeth the will of my Father which is in heaven.
>
> Many will say to me in that day, Lord, Lord, have we not prophesied in thy name? and in thy name have cast out devils? and in thy name done many wonderful works?
>
> And then will I profess unto them, I never knew you: depart from me, ye that work iniquity. (Matt. 7:21–23)

Why does he say, "I never knew you?" Because these uncharitable individuals never knew *him*. In other words, Jesus taught that churches and their members who take upon themselves his name, make a baptism covenant with him, and practice the beatitudes should not be interfered with by the Church, for they will receive "life eternal" and "inherit the kingdom."

It has been said that a person should not criticize their religious leaders, even if the criticism is true. In this respect, it is interesting that Jesus both praised and criticized his own religion and its leaders. In organizational religion, both the priestly and the prophetic spirits are needed. The priestly function brings stability and conserves the important values of the past. The prophetic role is progressive, interested in reforming the status quo and improving the future. For the priest, God *has* spoken; to the prophet, God *is* speaking.

While Jesus was more prophet than priest, he clearly recognized the contributions of both. He observed that, while churches play an important role in society, their tendency is to evolve in the direction of emphasizing institutional concerns over the needs of people. Jesus organized his church before his death (Matt. 16:18) but said little about organizational matters. He emphasized first the needs of individuals, then community and organizational needs. Church parties of his day had entirely reversed this order and saw no need to repent. He said, I can't put my "new wine into [your] old bottles" (the Jewish parties), or sew my "new cloth on an old garment" (Mark 2:21–22). The religious groups had lost their way and his new order restored their true purpose.

In Jesus' day religious life was unbalanced, excessively tipped toward the priestly influence. For instance, while Jesus associated with sinners and helped them, the priests avoided sinners and judged them. Jesus saw the church as a hospital for the sick, the Pharisees and Sadducees as a show place for the already righteous. Jesus viewed the Sabbath as made for the joy and healing of human beings; the Pharisees saw it as a system of rules that human beings must scrupulously follow out of guilt. Jesus focused on the spirit of the law; the scribes and Essenes on a strict interpretation of the law's letter. The Pharisees, who were by far the largest and most influential Jewish party, promulgated rules for governing daily life in every respect. In Jesus' day these rules had become "commandments," akin to scripture; Jesus called them "the traditions of the elders" and ignored most of this body of extra-scriptural policy and practice. Such minor "matters," he said, were like "strain[ing) at gnats" and should be left for *individuals* to decide (Matt. 15:2; Mark 7:5–8; Matt. 23:23–24).

If Jesus visited our various religious societies today, which of our prescriptions about behavioral minutia, to which we assign near-commandment status, would Jesus call "traditions of the elders"? Dictating and repeating a code of conduct for individual behavior on almost every occasion encourages Church members to engage in unrighteous judgement of others. Such judgement creates an atmosphere of tension, causing some to feel unaccepted. It is only natural that they would withdraw from our religious communities. In others it breeds hypocrisy, with people outwardly pretending conformity even while they secretly violate these near-commandments. The multiplication and emphasis of such rules blurs the distinction between significant commandments and trivial observances, making them seem of equal importance, especially among young people. Having observed these consequences first-hand during his formative years, Jesus rejected this approach to religion in his new church. He taught the things that mattered most and left the remainder to individual choice.

Time and again Jesus cautioned the religious communities of his day about elevating their institutional beliefs, rules, and rituals—"right beliefs"—to the stature of the "weightier matters of the law, judgment, mercy, and faith" (Matt. 12:1-7; 23:23). Jesus said these much-multiplied commandments, rules, and regulations made believers feel "heavy laden," while "my yoke is easy, and my burden is light" (Matt. 11:28-30). The tendency of churches, then and now, is to look beyond the mark, to require more than Jesus required for entering heaven. Thus, institutional beliefs and organizational needs often dominate worship, leaving all too little focus on Christ. Someone has observed that, when Jesus said, "I stand at the door and knock" (Rev. 3:20), he is outside asking to be let into one of his own churches.

Leaders in Christ's church should also make decisions about office and finances using the lens of Jesus' teachings, rather than through their own institutional eyes. Jesus strongly expressed disapproval of some social customs that had developed. He observed, for instance, that even though "all ye are brethren," some members were seated by rank in "the chief seats" or "the highest seats," had distinctive titles, and "walk[ed] in long robes" and distinctive hats (Matt. 23:8, 6; Luke 20:46). They used these and other marks of distinction to establish the importance of some members over others. Jesus rebuked those who "love[d] greetings in the markets" and expected to be treated with special privileges (Luke 20:46; Matt 23:7). His concern focused on the fact that all such institutional behaviors, rituals, rules, regulations, and social practices had a tendency to encourage believers to follow the rabbis, priests, and leaders, rather than focusing on him and his teachings.

Problems arise when we see Jesus through the eyes of a leader instead of seeing the leader through the eyes of Jesus. When a religious leader and Jesus disagree, whom should we follow? Jesus counsels us to replicate his servant-style leadership on all these matters: "For one is your Master, even Christ" (Matt. 23:8–11). Just as Jesus taught that all are equal under law; here he taught that all are equal in the Church.

Jesus' Equal Treatment of Women and Children

Unlike Jewish teachers of his day, Jesus had an intimate teaching association with women. His circle of closest followers included both men and women. Interestingly, only men—never women—failed Jesus. A good indication of his attitude of equality toward them and their potential is the episode at Jacob's well, when Jesus chose a morally flawed Samaritan woman to be the catalyst of spiritual resurgence among her own people. She became his first missionary (John 4:4–42).

His affirmative attitude and equality toward women also is seen when making known his greatest revelation—his own resurrection from the dead. He appeared first to Mary Magdalene and another Mary, rather than to Peter and the other apostles; thus, Jewish women, who were not considered competent as witnesses in court, became the first witnesses to the most important event in Christian and world history (Matt. 28:1–10; John 20:11–18; Luke 24:10) The modern equivalent of this action would be Christ's appearing first, at his second coming, to a small group of devoted women believers rather than to the First Presidency.

Jesus making time for children

We see Jesus' kind and gentle attitude toward children in the Gospel of Mark. Some parents brought their young children for Jesus to "touch them" but

> his disciples rebuked those that brought them.
>
> But when Jesus saw it, he was much displeased, and said unto them, Suffer the little children to come unto me, and forbid them not. . . .
>
> And he took them up in his arms, put his hands upon them, and blessed them. (Mark 10:13-16)

This incident not only shows that the Lord valued children highly—rhetoric with which we are all familiar in political and church speeches about "the family"—but that he actually had *time* for them.

Choose Spiritual Opportunity over the Mundane

The well-known episode of different choices made by the sisters, Mary and Martha, occurred at their Bethany home and centered on Martha. Jesus was their house guest; and at some point during the visit, Jesus began teaching. Judaism at that time did not provide an opportunity for women to discuss the scriptures. Mary, recognizing what a unique opportunity this was to talk with the Lord, "sat at Jesus' feet and heard his word." Martha criticized her for this decision, since she was preoccupied with her duties as a hostess to the point that she overlooked everything else. Jesus did not rebuke her. Instead, he simply observed that she was "cumbered about [with] much serving" (her domestic chores were burdensome) and noted that "thou are careful and troubled about many things." In contrast to the "much serving" (was Martha going all out to prepare many elaborate dishes?) Jesus explained that only "one thing" (possibly a single dish of simple food) "is needful." He then explained that "Mary hath chosen that good part" (Luke 10:38–42). Without scolding Martha, he suggested another way for her to define her responsibilities of hospitality, while complimenting Mary's decision to concentrate during his brief visit on spiritual things rather than temporal ones. Jesus is teaching us not to be so caught up in our own small worlds that we fail to partake of a significant spiritual opportunity when it arises.

This example does not represent a simple dichotomy between a spiritual woman and a worldly one. Martha was also a spiritual woman, as we know from the events associated with the death of Lazarus. It was Martha, not Mary, who first greeted Jesus after the death of Lazarus and who first bore the stirring testimony: "I believe that thou art the Christ, the Son of God, which should come into the world" (John 11:27).

Jesus' Attitude toward Riches

Jesus' basic attitude concerning riches was expressed in his injunction to "seek ye *first* the kingdom of God, and his righteousness; and all these things [if you desire them] shall be added unto you" (Matt. 6:33; emphasis mine). Jesus demonstrated this principle in his own life when he was tempted in the wilderness by Satan and chose his spiritual mission over "all the kingdoms of the world" (Luke 4:5). Jesus never personally sought riches, but neither did he denounce them. He simply said: "Ye cannot serve God and mammon" (Luke 16:13).

In other words, we must decide what is first in our life, worldly riches or the wealth of the heavenly city. Can we choose both? No, we must decide which comes first and which is second. In the parables of the treasure in the field and the pearl of great price, Jesus taught that for "the kingdom of heaven" we must be willing to sacrifice "all" to obtain it (Matt. 13:44–46).

Jesus gave perhaps the best advice on the proper versus the improper use of riches in the Gospel of Luke. He began with the parable of the foolish rich man who decided to build many barns:

> The ground of a certain rich man brought forth plentifully:
>
> And he thought within himself, saying, What shall I do, because I have no room where to bestow my fruits?
>
> And he said, This will I do: I will pull down my barns, and build greater; and there will I bestow all my fruits and my goods.
>
> And I will say to my soul, Soul, thou hast much goods laid up for many years; take thine ease, eat, drink, and be merry.
>
> But God said unto him, Thou fool, this night thy soul shall be required of thee: then whose shall those things be, which thou hast provided?
>
> So is he that layeth up *treasure for himself*, and is not rich toward God. (Luke 12:16–21; emphasis mine)

Notice the frequent use of the word "I" in this parable. Jesus condemns the man, not because he is rich, but because he is selfish and proud. His priorities are imbalanced. The parable shows that material goods can make slaves out of us, taking all of our time to care for them, absorbing all of our attention, and thus allowing worldly things to choke out spiritual things.

Jesus continued his instructions in Luke 12, revealing the four responsibilities of a person possessing riches who wishes to enter the kingdom of heaven and therefore wish to use them properly. First, "seek ye the kingdom of God." Second, "sell that ye have," or, in other words, sell or give away the things that you are not using. Simplify your life. Don't accumulate simply for the sake of wealth, like the rich man and his barns. Third, "give alms"—that is, donate money, time, and talents for charitable purposes. Fourth, "provide yourselves bags which wax not old, a treasure in the heavens that faileth not"

(Luke 12:31, 33; cf. 1 Tim. 6:17–19). By this I think Jesus means that we should "invest" the riches to benefit and serve others. Use them to make eternal friends rather than being like the rich man who "layeth up treasure for himself" (Luke 12:21). Use it to motivate, inspire, and help others. Use the money for bonding and creating family memories. Jesus concludes by stating the reason for this action: "For where your treasure is, there will your heart be also" (v. 34).

Jesus' Views on Marriage and Divorce

Jesus' fundamental commandment about marriage was: what "God hath joined together, let not man put asunder" (Matt. 19:6). While the scriptures never state that Jesus himself was married, there was no reason to believe, according to Jewish law and custom, that he was not. He believed in the sacred nature of this union and accordingly expected those under a covenant of marriage to work at improving their relationship.

His instructions are perhaps even more relevant today than in his own times. When marriages were troubled, he clearly counseled repentance and reconciliation rather than divorce. He observed that Moses granted divorce in his day only "because of the hardness of your hearts . . . but from the beginning it was not so." When a marriage does end, Jesus asks that we get "a writing of divorcement," signalling the formal end of the marriage. Treating the union as something that can simply be walked away from unilaterally or negated by indifference means that the next union will be committing adultery. He also instructed that divorce, when it is inevitable, should be for a serious reason—he uses the example of adultery—rather than for "every [or any] cause" (Matt. 5:31–32; Matt. 19:3–9; cf. Mark 10:2–12; for Paul's view, see 1 Cor. 7). People who are not making a serious effort to save a troubled marriage are not practicing the Christian way.

Jesus' Personal Prayers

When praying, Jesus always addressed God intimately as "Father," "O my Father," "O righteous Father," "Holy Father," and "Abba [Dearest] Father" (John 17:1, 11, 25; Matt. 26:42; Mark 14:36; Rom. 8:15; Gal. 4:6). John 17:1–26 captures an intimate prayer episode, and the overwhelming message is about its personal nature. In this passage, he used more than 120 nouns and pronouns in speaking with his Father, as we shall later observe when quoting from some of these verses.

Jesus' intimate approach to prayer is unlike the formal declarations found in the Old Testament and among the religious leaders of his day. They prayed to "God," "the Lord," "the Holy One of Israel," "Redeemer of Israel," or "Lord of Hosts." Jesus' intimate prayers reveal his close relationship with his Father.

Meditation is a more advanced form of spiritual communication than merely repeating routine prayers. In this regard, Jesus has much to teach us. He usually prayed on a mountain or in a solitary place, sometimes communing all night with his Father (e.g., Matt. 14:23; Luke 5:16; 6:12; 9:18, 28; Mark 1:35; 6:46). When his need was urgent and distressing, such as when he was "in an agony, he prayed [even] more earnestly" (Luke 22:44).

The scriptural record shows that Jesus prayed frequently and diligently. He promised that "your heavenly Father [will] give the Holy Spirit to them that ask him" (Luke 11:13). Jesus often prayed for the Spirit and spiritual renewal. After "being baptized, and *praying* . . . the Holy Ghost descended . . . upon him." Thus, he was "full of the Holy Ghost" as he went forth "in the power of the Spirit into Galilee" and began his ministry (Luke 3:21–22; 4:1, 14; emphasis mine). In the Garden of Gethsemane, Jesus requested and received "strengthening" against the hour of his temptation—meaning the temptation to draw back from the isolation and agony of the atonement and crucifixion (Luke 22:42-43). After praying all night on another occasion, he came down from a mountain so renewed that he "healed them all." He was able to do this because "there went virtue out of him" (Luke 6:12, 19).

It should be a source of humility and strength to us that, like us, Jesus also frequently became depleted, or "poor in spirit," and sought renewal in private meditation and prolonged prayer. Asking for the Holy Spirit should also be paramount in our prayer life. I well remember that after each day's work at the Salt Lake County Jail of teaching, counseling, giving blessings, and hearing the most serious sins in the city, that I often felt "poor in spirit." On one occasion as I left the jail feeling emotionally exhausted and depleted, I silently offered up a simple prayer—not even in words so much as an expression of my weariness. I had not walked more than fifty feet from the jail doors when Christ's loving spirit renewed and replenished me to the point that I actually felt ready for another day. Under my breath I quietly said, "Thanks, Lord," and distinctly heard within my mind: "Thanks for doing my work." I relied on that amazing blessing for renewal for many days.

In his prayers, Jesus also requested guidance for his ministry and received instruction and inspiration about what he should say and do next. For example, on the Mount of Transfiguration, Jesus' prayer was answered by a physical transformation that enabled him to see not only Moses and Elijah, but also the Father. In that context, he received instruction about and needed strength for "his decease which he should accomplish at Jerusalem" (Luke 9:28-36, esp. 31). Jesus stated on several occasions that "I speak these things" only "as my Father hath taught me" (John 8:28). "The Father which sent me, he gave me a commandment, what I should say, and what I should speak" (John 12:49). And again, "The Son can do nothing of himself, but what he seeth the Father do: for what things soever he doeth, these also doeth the Son . . . [the Father] sheweth him all things that himself doeth" (John 5:19–20). As disciples, we too have a right to ask the Father for direction in our life's mission.

Jesus often made very specific requests on behalf of others. He asked, for example, that Peter's "faith fail not" (Luke 22:32) and that his Father would forgive the Roman soldiers who were crucifying him (Luke 23:34).

Of peculiar poignancy are the unanswered prayers, when he begged "with strong crying and tears" that he might escape the cross and live (Heb. 5:7; Matt. 26:39; Mark 14:35; Luke 22:42) and then implored his Father to know why he was abandoned alone on the cross (Mark 15:34; cf. Ps. 22:1–2, 16–19; Matt. 27:46).

Jesus' only recorded detailed prayer is in John 17, and nearly all of it is devoted to requests to bless his apostles and future believers:

> I pray for them [apostles] . . .
> That they may be one, as we are . . .
> Keep them from . . . evil. . . .
> Sanctify them through thy truth: thy word is truth. . . .
> Neither pray I for these [apostles] alone, but for them also [ancient and modern disciples) which shall believe on me through their word;
> That they all may be one; as thou, Father, art in me, and I in thee, that they also may be one in us. . . .
> That the love wherewith thou [Father) hast loved me may be *in* them, and *I in them.* (John 17:9, 11, 15, 17, 20–21, 26; emphasis mine)

This last request is that the Father will bestow upon them the Second Comforter. (See also John 14:21–23.)

Jesus also taught his disciples to pray, and the list of topics on which he encourages their prayers is revealing. They should pray for the kingdom of heaven to come, for daily necessities, for forgiveness, and for the strength to resist temptation and evil (Matt. 6:5–13). Jesus sometimes thanks his Father in advance for fulfilling his own requests, especially miracles (John 11:41; Mark 8:1–9; cf. Matt. 15:36–38; Matt. 14:15–21; cf. Luke 9:12–17). He also prays in gratitude to his Father that his disciples have received the truth (Matt. 11:25–26; cf. Luke 10:21) and in his blessing the emblems of the sacrament (Matt. 26:26–27; cf. Mark 14:22–24).

Jesus' Perspective on his Second Advent

The disciples asked Jesus: "What shall be the sign[s] of thy coming, and of the end of the world?" (Matt. 24:3). Without hesitation, he answered with a concise outline of the essential signs in this order (Matt. 24:23–39; Mark 13:4, 21–37; Luke 21:25–36):

1. Just before his second advent, there "shall arise false Christs, and false prophets, and shall shew great signs and wonders," deceiving many (Matt. 24:24).

2. Then will occur "the tribulation," also called "the abomination of desolation" and "the abomination that maketh desolate" (Matt. 24:15, 29; Dan. 11:31; 12:11). Jerusalem will come under siege before his return, just as it did in A.D. 70. The most detailed outline of events just prior to this tribulation and Christ's return is in Zechariah 12–14.

3. "Immediately after the tribulation of those days shall the sun be darkened, and the moon shall not give her light, and the stars shall fall from heaven, and the powers of the heavens shall be shaken." There will be "distress of nations" and "the sea and the waves roaring; men's hearts failing them for fear" (Matt. 24:29; Luke 21:25–26; cf. Joel 2:10, 30–31; Rev. 6:12–17; 8–10:4).

4. "And then shall appear the sign of the Son of man in heaven: and then shall all the tribes of the earth mourn, and

they shall see the Son of man coming in the clouds of heaven with power and great glory" (Matt. 24:30).

Expanding on the fourth point, Zechariah states:

His feet [the Messiah's] shall stand in that day upon the mount of Olives. (Zech. 14:4)
They shall look upon me whom they have pierced, and they shall mourn . . .
The land shall mourn . . .
All the families that remain, every family apart. (Zech. 12:10, 12, 14)
And one shall say unto him, What are these wounds in thine hands? Then he shall answer, Those with which I was wounded in the house of my friends. (Zech. 13:6)

John repeats that Jesus "cometh with clouds; and every eye shall see him, and they also which pierced him: and all kindreds of the earth shall wail because of him" (Rev. 1:7).

"The sign of [the coming of] the son of man" is thus twofold: First, Jesus will return to the Mount of Olives just as he left the Mount of Olives at his ascension, in the clouds of heaven (Acts 1:12, 9–11) and (2) multitudes will witness the wounds of his crucifixion, which shall cause great weeping among the believing and unbelieving.

Jesus provided a general sign of his coming by saying that just "as the days of Noe [Noah] were, so shall also the coming of the Son of man be"—that is: "The earth also was [morally] corrupt before God, and the earth was filled with violence" (Matt. 24:37; Gen. 6:11). He did not identify the exact time of his return, specifying that not even the angels in heaven have that information (Mark 13:32) but suggested that it lay far in the future when he told his ancient disciples that "the kingdom of heaven is as a man [Jesus] traveling into a *far country* . . . [and] *after a long time* the lord of those servants cometh, and reckoneth with them." The actual second coming, however, will be quick, like "lightning" coming "out of the east" (Matt. 25:14–19; 24:27; emphasis mine).

Jesus did not focus on the signs of his advent but instead on the preparation for it that his disciples should engage in: "Be not troubled," he encouraged them. "Watch ye therefore, and pray always, that ye may be accounted worthy to escape all these things [signs] that shall come to pass" (Matt. 24:6, 42; Luke 21:36). "The great and dreadful day of the Lord," is, as the saying goes, great for those who "know" him, but dreadful for those who don't (Mal. 4:5).

The entire chapter of Matthew 25 emphasizes preparation for his second advent. Jesus says, for example, "The kingdom of heaven is likened unto ten virgins . . . five of them were wise, and five were foolish." To the foolish, Jesus declared, "I know you not. Watch therefore, for ye know neither the day nor the hour wherein the Son of man cometh" (Matt. 25: 1–2, 12–13).

Authors writing entire books on this subject of necessity quote beyond Jesus and the scriptures. They have much to say, usually focusing not on preparation for his advent, but rather on the signs. This focus often has the effect of producing the emotions of fear, doom, and dread—all of them incompatible with love. "Love casteth out fear" (1 John 4:18).

Jesus' Leadership Style and Teaching

The twelve men whom Jesus chose as apostles demonstrated the strength of his leadership. Peter was strong willed, and Jesus called James and John "the sons of thunder," presumably because of their aggressive temperament (Mark 3:17; 10:35–37, 41; Luke 9:52–56). Matthew was a publican or tax collector for Rome, surely not a job in ancient Palestine for the shy and retiring; and Simon was a member of the Zealot party which was strongly opposed to Roman authority over the Jews, especially taxation (Matt. 10:3; Luke 6:15; Acts 1:13). Early

Quorum of the Twelve meetings were undoubtedly very interesting. Only a strong leader like Jesus would choose such diverse personalities to serve with him and be able to focus their energies on the ministry instead of dealing constantly with bickering and schism.

Medieval art tends to portray a physically frail, dreamy-eyed, and ineffectual Jesus. This depiction obviously stands in contradiction to the details from the scriptures that show Jesus as energetic, charismatic, able to speak for hours to crowds of thousands, and physically able to walk for days over rough country routes. It is unlikely that a physically feeble and other-worldly Jesus could hold the allegiance of four strong-willed fishermen and other diverse personalities. From the Galilee to Judea is a distance of over eighty miles each way, and Jesus repeatedly made that trip on foot. His physical stamina was also apparent in his ability to survive the ordeal of scourging, even after the sleepless night of agony in Gethsemane, followed by "bearing his cross" or crossbar part way to Calvary (John 19:1, 17; cf. Luke 23:26).

Jesus was and is an excellent leader because he had a vision, a well-defined purpose, and an organized method of accomplishing it. His vision plainly teaches us how to receive the rewards of the abundant life in mortality and eternal life in the next. The suitability of his style of leadership to achieve his purposes was clearly revealed when James and John asked him to make them the greatest in his kingdom, and to occupy the seats on his right and left hand. He instructed them that in *his* kingdom, the "greatest of all" is the "servant of all" (Mark 10:35–37, 41–45; Matt. 23:10–12; Luke 22:24–27). This picture stands the world's pyramid of greatness on its head. In worldly terms, the "greatest" individual occupies the top of the pyramid with everyone else supporting him. Unquestionably, in God's pyramid, Jesus is the greatest, but he is at the bottom, serving and upholding all others. As an example of this servant-style leadership, Jesus washed the feet of his apostles (John 13:4–17). Later on, these men not only spent their lives in sharing the news of his ministry with others but voluntarily laid down their lives for him.

Being able to inspire lasting love in human beings is the most difficult thing in the world for a leader, which is why so many default swiftly to the surer, though temporary, use of power. Alexander, Caesar, Charlemagne, Napoleon, Hitler, Stalin, Hussein, and countless others have founded empires on force and fear. Some of them also had visions that temporarily inspired the masses to follow them, but such inspiration did not outlast their own lives. Their empires did not last. Jesus founded his kingdom on love. Now, two thousand years later, millions bear his name, and many are willing to live daily lives in conformity with his teachings and also die for him. The eternal kingdom of Christ is increasingly proclaimed over all the earth, teaching an inspiring message of sacrificial love and joy.

A good leader is also a great teacher and a sterling example. We see evidence for this in how we view Jesus. We do not think of him as the administrator or CEO of the Christian movement, but rather as a teacher. Jesus was—and is—a great teacher because he was morally good, because he was close to his Father, and because he cared. He cared passionately about doing what was just and right for the individual. He was motivated by mercy and love. He engaged the mind of his listeners, taught with the Spirit, and made the scriptures come alive. Jesus appealed to the best within his listeners, constantly inviting them to the great supper, the abundant life. He never used fear or compulsion as a motivator and seldom used duty as a method of persuasion. Rather, Jesus appealed with love, building faith by promising the blessings that would be received by those who came to him and followed him.

As a teacher he used current events, the common objects, or familiar processes in his environment to make his points clear. He sometimes challenged accepted religious and historical teachings, traditions, and patterns of behavior. To his believing disciples, he freely and plainly gave the words of life. He answered their questions and helped them understand his meaning, encouraging them to ponder and come to their own conclusions.

However, in a large crowd where contentious critics mingled with believers, he usually taught in parables. This method provided both a simple story as the entrance to understanding but made available a deeper meaning for those who were already believers. His enemies thus could not "catch him in his words" (Mark 12:13) and bring him to a Jewish court for punishment.

When interacting with hostile critics, Jesus advised being "wise as serpents, and harmless as doves" (Matt. 10:16). He demonstrated this technique when a woman taken in adultery was brought before him, with the sole purpose being to ensnare him in a no-win argument. The Law of Moses required the death penalty for adultery, but Roman law forbade a sentence of death in such cases. Her accusers asked Jesus, "What sayest thou?", confidently expecting that Jesus would be trapped as a lawbreaker no matter what he said. If Jesus upheld either law, they could charge him with advocating disrespect for the other. The accusers were being officious, for it was not their business to charge or judge the woman, but rather that of the spouse and the judges.[1] They had neither a lawful nor a moral right to intervene. Jesus sidestepped the dilemma with his answer: "He that is without sin among you, let him first cast a stone at her." One by one they slunk away (John 8:3–11).

Another example of how Jesus combined being "wise" and "harmless" is the incident of paying the much-hated Roman tax. Jewish leaders, seeking to destroy Jesus, hoped to trap him into an answer that they could construe as rebellion and then turn him over to the Roman authorities. They chose a coin stamped with the image of Caesar purposely, hoping to provoke a reply which would identify Jesus with the Zealots who refused to pay taxes because the coins bore a "graven image" (Exod. 20:4). For the Jews, God was king, and paying tribute to the image or kingship of any other ruler—though a fact of political life—was a violation of their monotheism.

Thus, the questioners asked Jesus: "Is it lawful to give tribute to Caesar, or not?" If Jesus answered no, he would be more popular but subject to immediate arrest and probably to execution by Roman authorities. If he answered yes, he would lose popularity with the Jews. He answered:

> Shew me the tribute money. . . .
> Whose is this image and superscription?
> They say unto him, Caesar's. Then saith he unto them, Render therefore unto Caesar the things which are Caesar's; and unto God the things that are God's. (Matt. 22:17, 19–21)

His listeners "marvelled" at his answer, then "left him" (v. 22). They probably expected a yes or no answer but instead Jesus taught them a correct principle—namely, that paying taxes was not violating God's commandments. Then he let his surprised audience work out for themselves how to apply it.

To those who were openly his enemies, Jesus responded to their questions with questions that turned the argument back on them. After cleansing the temple of moneychangers, his enemies demanded:

> By what authority doest thou these things? . . .
> And Jesus answered and said unto them, I will also ask of you one question, and answer me, and I will tell you by what authority I do these things.

Jesus then asked whether John the Baptist's baptism was "from heaven, or of men?" After some worried discussion, they answered, "We cannot tell." (Interestingly, they did not try Jesus' tactic of sidestepping the question—they simply sidestepped the answer.) Jesus said, then: "Neither do I tell you by what authority I do these things" (Mark 11:28-33).

In short, Christian disciples can learn from Jesus' example how to be both a leader and a teacher in his kingdom.

Conclusion

On the final Sunday of his life, Jesus began his entry into Jerusalem for the feast of the Passover, in meekness, riding upon an ass. "And as he went, they [the people] spread their clothes in the way." Upon becoming visible "at the descent of the mount of Olives, the whole multitude of the disciples began to rejoice and praise God with a loud voice for all the mighty works that they had seen; Saying, Blessed be the King that cometh in the name of the Lord" (Luke 19:36-40). Jesus was truly triumphant in overcoming the world, a triumph of his incomparable character and ministry. The multitude knew that he was the Christ and could not be constrained from praise and worship.

The thirteen examples cited in this chapter are perhaps enough of a thumbnail sketch to reveal the character of Jesus: We see his sense of fair play and rejection of privilege. We perceive his choice of the spiritual life over worldliness, also, his affirmation that spiritual opportunities should take priority over mundane cares. We detect his great respect for each person's free agency and his or her right to choose. We have also seen that he often chooses to intervene in our struggles after the trial of our faith. We notice his love for others and his graciousness in allowing others to love him. We see him empathetically share the burdens of others. We discern his respect for women and children and his willingness to spend time with them. We observe that he holds the marriage covenant sacred. We see his concise and straightforward teachings about his second advent, emphasizing the need for believers to prepare for it rather than emphasizing the fearfulness of the coming signs. We understand his intimate relationship with the Father, maintained by constant prayer. We note his great gifts as a servant-style leader and as a teacher. The Apostle Paul could have been using the character of Jesus when he describes the nature of charity in his epistle to the Corinthians (slightly modified in this quotation):

>Jesus suffereth long, and he is kind; Jesus envieth not; Jesus vaunteth not himself, and is not puffed up.
>
>Jesus doth not behave himself unseemly, seeketh not his own.
>
>Jesus is not easily provoked.
>
>Jesus thinketh no evil. Jesus rejoiceth not in iniquity, but he rejoiceth in the truth: Jesus beareth all things, believeth all things, hopeth all things, and endureth all things.
>
>Jesus never faileth. (1 Cor. 13:4-8)

ഇന്ദ

Note

1. J. R. Dummelow, *A Commentary on the Holy Bible* (New York: Macmillan, 1971), 788.

Chapter 5

The Meaning of Atonement

Jesus came to earth to teach us how to live. By taking upon ourselves his nature, we become at-one with him and live "more abundantly" (John 10:10). Jesus also came to die and to resurrect from the dead, giving us hope of our own resurrection. Because he did so, he gained the power to "draw all men" to follow him, become like him, and dwell again with him in the celestial city of God.

The opening two chapters of the Bible describe the Garden of Eden and the last two describe the heavenly city of God. It appears that the Garden of Eden was patterned after the Garden "in the midst of the paradise [city] of God" (Rev. 2:7). For example, both environments reveal a pattern where divine harmony exists and where discord is not known. Moral and intellectual darkness, disease, and death are not found. In both places, premortal man and Adam and Eve walk and talk with God. The spiritual estrangement that now characterizes our mortal experience was unknown. Moreover, the situation of Adam and Eve in Eden, and the decision they were called upon to make, appears to parallel the figurative situation but real decision facing all premortal spirits in the city of God.

Belief in the pre-earth life of humankind helps to make sense of the fall of humankind (John 9:2; Acts 17:28; Rom.

8:29; Jude 1:6; Rev. 12:7–9; Jer. 1:5; Eph. 1:4; Ps. 82:6; D&C 49:17; D&C 93:23, 29). God's first instruction to Adam and Eve in Eden was to multiply and replenish the earth, i.e., to marry and have children. To do so, they had to violate his second instruction—not to partake of the tree of knowledge of good and evil. In other words, they needed to fully experience the law of opposites so that they could grow (Gen. 1:27–28; 2:16–17; 3:2–7). They and all premortal spirits in the city of God had to make choices about these two situations. To experience both conditions required a mortal experience on earth. With faith and courage, Adam, Eve, and all of us came to mortality. Adam and Eve heroically carried out *our* will and in so doing provided a mortal birth opportunity for all humanity.

Their decision, called a "transgression" (1 Tim. 2:14; Gen. 3:6; Moses 6:59), and our own decision to come to mortality was not a sin. Instead the announced consequences were designed in God's wisdom "for thy sake." As God said: "Thou shalt surely die," physically and spiritually. A persistent theological dilemma has always been why, given the desirability of growth, God should have given two commandments, the keeping of one of which required the breaking of the other. I hypothesize that God, perhaps to protect himself, counseled Adam and Eve not to partake of mortality (Gen. 3:17; 2:16–17). He apparently wanted them and us to feel the full weight of our moral choice to participate in mortal life. Like the entire human race, Adam and Eve were not compelled to come to the earth and experience mortality. Thus, if we fail to return to the heavenly city, we cannot blame God because putting ourselves in a situation necessary for our progression was and had to be our free choice.

Our progression from heaven meant that we would receive a physical body which would experience the dissolution process of death. Leaving the heavenly city for mortality also meant being without open and unveiled spiritual guidance. The

"And I will fasten him as a nail in a sure place"(Isa. 22:23)

Father appointed Jesus Christ to solve these two problems. He gave Jesus enormous power—the keys of the resurrection and the right to assign each individual to a post-mortal kingdom or station. But before the Father gave Jesus these powers, Jesus had to prove worthy of the Father's trust by passing his Father's test. He first agreed to represent the Father's character and personality in mortal life and thus became the revelation of God to the world to teach all people how to live.

The second part of Christ's test was the depth of his love for us. Jesus passed this test by voluntarily giving up his life. This was no easy or trivial test. Jesus pled: "Father, if it be possible, let this cup pass from me: nevertheless not as I will, but as thou wilt" (Matt. 26:36-39; cf. Luke 22:42-44). The Apostle Paul noted that Jesus "offered up [these] prayers and supplications with strong crying and tears unto him that was able to save him from death," but the Father said no (Heb. 5:7). This is apparently the Son's only request that the Father refused to grant. Jesus possessed the power to avoid arrest and death but instead voluntarily embraced them. When Jesus was arrested at the Mount of Olives, Peter drew his sword and cut off the ear of a member of the arresting party. Jesus replaced it, healed it, then asked Peter instructionally: "Thinkest thou that I cannot now pray to my Father, and [receive] . . . more than twelve legions [72,000!] of angels"? He continued, "But how then shall the scriptures be fulfilled"—regarding his betrayal, arrest, crucifixion, and resurrection[1]—"that thus *it must be*"? (Ps. 91:11-12; Matt. 26:51-54; emphasis mine).

The Apostle John defines love as the willingness to die for another (John 15:13; 1 John 3:16). Love is not satisfied until it has made every sacrifice within its power. No more complete sacrifice can be imagined than those of honor, ease, and finally life. For when an individual lays down his or her life for a cause or for a friend, he or she has given all he or she has to give. Beyond that point, there is nothing more to give. Jesus voluntarily gave his life, in the faith that his Father would resurrect him from the dead three days later as promised. There is simply no greater act of faith, obedience, sacrifice, love, and consecration found in all of scripture. And for this pure act of faith, obedience, sacrifice, love, and consecration, Jesus proved that he was worthy of the Father's complete confidence. Having shown himself trustworthy to the utmost, Jesus then received the keys of judgement from the Father. This endowment included the enormous powers of resurrection and assigning kingdoms to all humanity. The Father granted this power to his Son only when he knew (and perhaps more importantly, when Jesus himself knew) that Jesus could be trusted with such power.

> For as the Father raiseth up the dead, and quickeneth them; even so the Son quickeneth [will soon quicken] whom he will.
> For the Father judgeth no man, but hath committed [will soon commit] all judgement unto the Son . . .
> For as the Father hath life in himself; so hath he given [will soon give] to the Son to have life in himself;
> And hath given [will soon give] him authority to execute judgment . . .
> And [all] shall come forth; they that have done good, unto the resurrection of life; and they that have done evil, unto the resurrection of damnation. (John 5:21–22, 26–27, 29)

After his resurrection, Jesus confirmed: "All power is given unto me in heaven and in earth" (Matt. 28:18). As the epistle to the Hebrews explains: "Being made perfect, he became the author of eternal salvation unto all them that *obey him*" (Heb. 5:9; emphasis mine). "Know me" is what Jesus asks of us which, in reality, is to truly follow *him* (John 8:19; 1 John 2:3; 4:7). He alone determines our suitability for the city of God, for "no man cometh unto the Father, but by me." He is "the keeper of the gate . . . and he employeth no servant there" (John 14:6; 2 Ne. 9:41). Our debt to him is immeasurable. Yet the Lord, in his parable of the unmerciful servant, clearly teaches that he will be merciful to us in the judgement when we have shown mercy to our fellow human beings (Matt. 18:23-35).

There is a second important reason why Jesus had to die voluntarily. Sterling M. McMurrin, who was E. E. Distinguished Professor of Philosophy at the University of Utah, has stated, as have others, that no facet of Christianity has been more difficult to understand than the reason human salvation depends on the death of Christ. He summarizes: "Four major conceptions of the atonement can be discerned in the development of Christian theology, and today the overtones of all four, together with their language and imagery, are common-place in the Christian Church. They can be roughly designated as the substitution, ransom, satisfaction, and moral theories, in accordance with the order of their historical appearance. Each can justifiably claim some scriptural support."[2]

McMurrin then describes each of these four historical models. The substitution theory maintains that Christ's sinless death was a substitute for the punishment that human beings deserved because of their sins. Without Christ's (substitute) death, the sinner would have been punished not only for the consequences of Adam's decision to come to mortality, but for "Adam's sin" itself.[3]

According to the ransom theory, human beings fell under Satan's dominion because of Adam's sin. God purchases human souls from the devil, using Christ's death as the purchase price or ransom. Satan agreed to this bargain because he believed he would have power over Christ after he released human souls from death. But after the transaction is completed, Satan fails because he cannot keep a divine and perfect soul (Christ) in captivity.[4]

The satisfaction theory maintains that God is a being of absolute justice and absolute mercy. Thus, Adam's sin broke a law that offended God's honor. He therefore demanded satisfaction. Christ's sinless death, accepted because of his great mercy for us, compensated, mended, repaired, or satisfied the law broken in Eden.[5]

The moral theory maintains that Christ must die and resurrect from the dead for the moral improvement of humankind. Christ's voluntary sacrifice and his resurrection moves us to a consciousness of guilt; hence, we repent and effect a moral change of life which eliminates the need for punishment.[6]

It is little wonder that modern Christian worshippers are confused, especially when several of these theories, which are logically incompatible, are commingled in the hymns we sing, the sermons we hear, and many of the books we read. The modern Christian thus concludes that the Atonement of Christ is a concept so complicated that it is virtually impossible to grasp.

While all four of these traditional explanations are identified in scripture, the moral theory is more convincing and far simpler. In John 12, Jesus clearly explains why he must die. He said:

> Except a corn [kernel] of wheat fall into the ground and die, it abideth alone: but if it dies [and then comes alive again], it bringeth forth much fruit. . . .
> And I, if I be lifted up from the earth [i.e., die upon the cross], will [by my resurrection and ascension] draw all men unto me. (John 12: 24, 32)

Like the grain of wheat that dies, then comes alive and "bringeth forth much fruit," so will Jesus' resurrection from the dead "draw all men unto me." A child can understand that, when a single grain of wheat is planted in a small cup, it will sprout and eventually produce many more grains of wheat. In the same way, Jesus' resurrection depends on his death. Without the resurrection, Christianity would have gradually ceased to become viable except to the extent that the moral beauty of his teachings continued to inspire others. It is Christ's resurrection from the dead that validates his words and ministry, including his promise that we ourselves will rise from the dead (1 Pet. 1:3, 21). It is the evidence of and belief in his resurrection that "draws" people to his life, character, and his vision of the kingdom of heaven. Christ came to earth to resolve the consequences of Adam and Eve's decision of coming to mortality (physical and spiritual death), not to "pay" for Adam's so-called sin. Believing that we human beings wanted to come to earth and that God also desired us to have this experience of growth makes the substitution, ransom, and satisfaction theories of why Christ had to die irrelevant. In other words, human life is not a sin and is not caused by a sin. Hence, no substitute sacrifice was required. There was no need to pay off the devil (ransom); or to satisfy the alleged offense to God's honor.

Jesus began to "draw all men unto me" by reconverting his apostles who had denied and forsaken him at his crucifixion. John was the first apostle who believed that Jesus had been resurrected from the dead (John 20:1-10). According to the Gospel of John, Mary Magdalene arrived at the tomb early Easter morning, found it open and empty, assumed that the body had been stolen, and reported her sorrowful conclusion to Peter and John. When the two apostles entered the tomb, they saw the undisturbed grave clothes, lying where Jesus' body had been. This sight left Peter "wondering in himself at that which was [had] come to pass" (Luke 24:12). John, however, was more perceptive. "He saw [the unwound clothes] and believed" that Jesus had risen from the dead (John 20:6-9). Significantly, John was also the first to recognize the risen Lord on the shore of Lake Galilee (John 21:7).

Jesus' torso and limbs had been tightly bound in layers of cloth after "the manner of the Jews"—just as Lazarus's body had been—with a resinous gum called "myrrh" placed between the various layers, yet the clothing remained undisturbed (John 19:39-40; John 11:44). The layers of cloth wrapped around Jesus' body kept their shape, only collapsing in on themselves when the body moved out from their layers. No one had unwrapped the body from the coverings and stolen it away; tomb robbers would have taken the valuable linen and myrrh with them. Or if, for some reason, they decided not to, they would not have taken the time to rearrange the linen so that it looked as if it still wrapped a corpse. Neither had the severely wounded Jesus revived, disentangled himself from the wrappings, rolled the stone away from the inside, eluded the guards, and wandered away.

No, the body was simply missing. Something had happened to the body of Jesus, giving it new and remarkable powers. The body had emerged from the grave clothes leaving them in one piece. It was not the *empty tomb* that aroused faith in John and perhaps Peter, but the position in which the linen clothes lay.

Jesus, however, knew that his resurrection from the dead required much stronger evidence than his disappearance from intact grave clothes. On Easter evening, he appeared to ten of his frightened apostles, even though the doors were locked, and said: "Behold my hands and my feet, that it is I myself: handle me, and see; for a spirit hath not flesh and bones, as ye see me have. And when he had thus spoken, he shewed them his hands and his feet" (Luke 24:39-40). A week later, Jesus again appeared to this group of men and the Apostle Thomas, who had been absent the previous week. Thomas also saw and touched Christ's wounds. John later summarized their

Thomas: "My Lord and my God" (John 20:28).

several experiences: "We have seen with our eyes, which we have looked upon, and our hands have handled, of the Word of life" (John 20:24-28; 1 John 1:1).

Luke, in the Book of Acts, records that for "many days" the resurrected Christ "shewed himself alive after his passion by many infallible proofs, being seen of them [the apostles and others] forty days," after which at Jerusalem, he ascended into heaven before their eyes (Acts 13:31; 1:1-9). Peter said of these days, Jesus

> raised up the third day, and shewed him[self] openly;
> Not to all the people, but unto witnesses chosen before of God, even to us, who did eat and drink with him after he rose from the dead. (Acts 10:40-41)

Eating, drinking, touching the wounds of Christ, and watching him ascend into heaven indicates that the apostles and others did not see either a phantom or resuscitated Jesus, but rather an embodied resurrected being. Listing those who had "seen" the resurrected Christ during the forty-day ministry, Paul wrote that Jesus "was seen of Cephas [Peter], then of the twelve: After that, he was seen of above five hundred brethren at once; of whom the greater part remain [alive] unto this present, but some are fallen asleep." Paul wrote 1 Corinthians in about A.D. 55, before the four Gospels were written. Thus twenty-two years after Christ resurrected from the dead (ca. A.D. 33), most of this group of more than 500 witnesses to the risen Christ were still alive. Paul was issuing an open invitation to the church at Corinth to talk with these witnesses and evaluate their testimony. Knowing Paul's inquisitive nature, he had probably taken this step himself. Paul continued: "After that, he was seen of James: then of all the apostles. And last of all he was seen of me" (1 Cor. 15:5-8). James was the unbelieving brother of Jesus, who converted after seeing his resurrected brother.

James became an apostle and is believed to have been a leader in the church at Jerusalem (Gal. 1:19; Mark 6:3; cf. John 7:3-5).

Shortly after Jesus ascended to heaven, the apostles replaced Judas in the Quorum of Twelve. They determined that the new apostle had to have witnessed Jesus' entire ministry, crucifixion, resurrection, and ascension. As Peter put it, the new apostle must have been "with us all the time that the Lord Jesus went in and out among us, beginning from the baptism of John, unto that same day that he was taken up [ascended] from us." As a second requirement, the new apostle "must . . . be ordained to be a witness with us of his resurrection" (Acts 1:21-23). Thus Barsabas and Matthias, the two men the eleven apostles were considering to replace Judas, were also "a witness . . . of his resurrection," crucifixion, ascension, and ministry. Peter later wrote of these events: "We have not followed cunningly devised fables . . . but were eyewitnesses of his majesty" (2 Pet. 1:16). The resurrection of Christ is one of the best documented spiritual events in scripture, with nearly two dozen witnesses identified by name and more than five hundred in the Galilee area.

It was the evidence of a risen Christ that turned these apostles, who had been denying and despairing at the time of Christ's crucifixion, into the greatest and most aggressive missionary force in history. Now one third of the earth's inhabitants believe in Christ. Before the crucifixion, the apostles feared Roman and Jewish authority; after the resurrection, they become audacious and fearless teachers. For instance, very soon after the day of Christ's ascension, a large crowd assembled at Jerusalem for the Feast of Pentecost. Certainly many of these participants had heard reports about the resurrected Christ and wished to learn more about such an extraordinary claim. Speaking for the twelve, Peter boldly addressed the audience: "Jesus hath God raised up, whereof we all are witnesses." Convinced by Peter's firm testimony, many "gladly received his word [and] were baptized: and the same day there were added unto them about three thousand souls" (Acts 2:32, 41).

Peter "preached" soon after to an even larger audience on the "the resurrection [of Christ] from the dead." He testified: "God hath raised [Christ] from the dead; whereof we are witnesses. . . . [And] many of them which heard the word believed; and the number of the men was about five thousand" (Acts 4:2; 3:15; 4:4). Several verses later, all of the apostles, one after another, testified to another enormous crowd in Jerusalem: "And with great power gave the apostles [their] witness of the resurrection of the Lord Jesus. . . . And believers were the more added to the Lord, multitudes both of men and women" (Acts 4:33; 5:14). In sum, the effect on people when the apostles straightforwardly related their personal experiences with the risen Christ was nothing short of dramatic and life-changing.

Three times between these cited testimonies (Acts 2:32–5:42), the Jewish Sanhedrin had Peter, John, and the other apostles arrested, beaten, threatened with death, and arbitrarily ordered "not to speak at all nor teach in the name of Jesus" (Acts 4:17–18; 5:17–42). Ignoring the threats, "Peter and the other apostles" fearlessly testified to the Sanhedrin: "God . . . [hath] raised up Jesus. . . . And we are his witnesses" (Acts 5:29–30, 32). Less than two months earlier, Peter in the high priest's house had denied Jesus three times; now before large crowds and confronted by a battery of the chief priests, he would not be silent about Christ! In a few weeks the disciples in the Jerusalem area had grown from "an hundred and twenty" to about 15,000 (Acts 1:15).

Early descriptions of the resurrection narratives of Christ are phrased as reports of a literal/physical event. They remain literal and physical throughout the New Testament.[7] Evidence for the risen Christ was the central focus of missionary work in the early church as recorded in the book of Acts and in the epistles of the Apostle Paul, who repeatedly testified:

"Christ [is] risen from the dead, and become the firstfruits of them that slept" (1 Cor. 15:20). All these leader-witnesses were persecuted and eventually gave their lives for Christ.

Witnesses of the risen Christ inspired many other early Christians to endure persecution until their own martyrdom. Ignatius, the second bishop of Antioch in Syria, is an example. He was a contemporary of the Apostle John and perhaps also knew other apostles. He became a martyr in A.D. 110. In a letter to the church at Smyrna sometime before his death, Ignatius wrote: "He [Christ] was in the flesh even after the resurrection; and when He came to Peter and his company, He said to them, 'Lay hold and handle me, and see that I am' . . . and straightway they touched Him, and they believed. . . . And after His resurrection He ate with them and drank with them as one in the flesh."[8]

During the Last Supper, Jesus introduced the sacrament: "And as they were eating, Jesus took bread, and blessed it, and brake it, and gave it to the disciples . . . this is my body. And he took the cup . . . this is my blood" (Matt. 26:26–28). After the resurrection, Christ continued meeting with his disciples during meals, often with sacramental overtones. He appeared to his ten apostles "and did eat," and a week later to the eleven, "as they sat at meat" (Luke 24:42–43; Mark 16:14). On the shores of the Galilee, the risen Christ, "taketh bread, and giveth" it to the apostles (John 21:13). After joining two disciples on the road to Emmaus, while the risen Jesus "sat at meat with them, he took bread, and blessed it, and brake, and gave to them. And their eyes were opened, and they knew him." Not only did their "heart burn within," they knew unmistakably that Jesus was alive (Luke 24:30–32). In the Gospel of the Hebrews, a noncanonical Jewish Christian work, the risen Christ appeared to his brother James and said: "Bring a table and bread. . . . He [Jesus] took the bread and blessed it and brake it and gave it to James and called unto him: My brother,

"Do [this] in remembrance of me" (Luke 22:19)

eat thy bread, for the son of man is risen from among them that sleep."9 Did the resurrected Lord also visit "five hundred brethren at once" (1 Cor. 15:6) during a sacramental supper?

Early Christians understood that the risen Christ had appeared during meals and would return during their sacred meals.10 Jesus had explicitly promised the worthy: "Ye may eat and drink at my table" and "I will come in to him, and sup with him, and he with me" (Luke 22:30; Rev. 3:20). The apostles often reminded members to "eat this bread, and drink this cup . . . till he comes" (1 Cor. 11:26). "And they [the saints] continued steadfastly in the apostles' doctrine and fellowship, and in breaking of bread, and in prayers . . . continuing daily . . . breaking bread from house to house," anticipating not only his Spirit to be with them but a visit from the living Christ (Acts 2:42–46). Their empowering application of the atonement brought great strength and unity to the Christian community.

In our own modern era, David O. McKay has written: "Let the sacrament hour be one experience of the day in which the worshiper . . . commune[s] with his God. Great events have happened in this Church because of such communion."11 Imagine a service where Christ appears and invites all to see and touch, not the emblems, but of the seven marks of his atonement. Remarkable events have and will yet occur to individuals and congregations during this time of sacred remembrance.

The atonement of Christ is twofold. One aspect is his life and the other is his death. In the LDS prayer on the bread of the sacrament, we center our thoughts on Jesus as the Bread of Life and on his teachings, evaluating whether our daily walk harmonizes with his life. Here the prayer invokes the first part of Christ's atonement by affirming that those who partake are "*willing* to take upon them the name of thy Son, and always remember him [his character] and keep his commandments which he has given them" (D&C 20:77; emphasis mine). It is fitting for us during such moments to recommit ourselves to the beatitudes, remembering how Jesus lived them, or to focus on the nine qualities of Jesus that Peter and Paul identified (2 Pet. 1:4–8; Gal. 5:22–23). As our Christian ideals are tested by the trials of daily life during the week, we experience the promised blessing of the sacrament by having the prompting of "his Spirit" in our time of need.

In the sacramental prayer on the water, we center our thoughts on Christ's crucifixion but especially on his resurrection. Just as he arose from the dead on Sunday, so we commemorate him each Sunday. Those who take the water do so "in remembrance of the blood of thy Son, which was shed for them . . . [and promise to] always remember him"—especially his suffering sacrifice and his promise that he will return to us in glory. Such conscious remembering brings the promise that we may always "have his Spirit to be with" us (D&C 20:79).

෨෩ඣ

Notes

1. *The Betrayal:* "Mine own familiar friend, in whom I trusted, which did eat of my bread, hath lifted up his heel against me" (Ps. 41:9). "If ye think good, give me my price; and if not, forbear. So they weighed for my price thirty pieces of silver" (Zech. 11:12).

The Arrest: "They part my garments among them, and cast lots upon my vesture" (Ps. 22:18). "He was oppressed, and he was afflicted, yet he opened not his mouth: he is brought as a lamb to the slaughter, and as a sheep before his shearers is dumb, so he openeth not his mouth" (Isa. 53:7).

The Crucifixion: "My God, my God, why hast thou forsaken me? why art thou so far from helping me . . . the assembly of the wicked have inclosed me: they pierced my hands and my feet" (Ps. 22:1, 16). "And I will fasten him as a nail in a sure place; and he shall be for a glorious throne to his father's house" (Isa. 22:23). "He hath borne our griefs, and carried our sorrows . . . he was wounded for our transgressions, he was bruised for our iniquities . . . with his stripes we are healed . . . the Lord hath laid on him the iniquity of us all . . . he was taken from prison and . . . for the transgression of my people was he stricken. And he made his grave with the wicked, and with the rich in his death; because he had done no violence, neither was any deceit in his mouth . . . my righteous servant shall justify many . . . he hath poured out his soul unto death: and he was numbered with the transgressors; and he bare the sin of many, and made intercession for the transgressors" (Isa. 53:4-6, 8-12).

The Resurrection: "He will swallow up death in victory; and the . . . . dead . . . shall live, together with . . . [their] body shall they arise" (Isa. 25:8; 26:19). "And they shall look upon me whom they have pierced, and they shall mourn. . . . And one shall say unto him, What are these wounds in thine hands? Then he shall answer, Those with which I was wounded in the house of my friends" (Zech. 12:10; 13:6).

2. Sterling M. McMurrin, *The Theological Foundations of the Mormon Religion* (Salt Lake City: University of Utah Press, 1965), 84.

3. Ibid., 84, 88; 1 Thess. 1:10; 5:9-10; Gal. 1:4.

4. McMurrin, *The Theological Foundations of the Mormon Religion*, 85-86; Mark 10:45; 1 Tim. 2:6; 2 Ne. 9:5, 8-9.

5. McMurrin, *The Theological Foundations of the Mormon Religion*, 86-87, 90; Alma 42:14-15, 25; 34:15-16.

6. McMurrin, *The Theological Foundations of the Mormon Religion*, 88–89; John 12:24, 32; 1 Pet. 3:18; 3 Ne. 27:14–15.

7. The birth narratives of Jesus contain important discrepancies, but not those of the resurrection, which to me is the foundation of Christianity. A few researchers believe that the resurrection narratives evolved between the Gospel of Mark and John, becoming more impressive. For a scholarly refutation of this idea, see George Eldon Ladd, *I Believe in the Resurrection of Jesus* (Grand Rapids, MI: William B. Eerdmans Publishing, 1975), 79–103.

8. "The Epistles of St. Ignatius," translated and edited by J. R. Harmer, in J. B. Lightfoot, *The Apostolic Fathers* (Grand Rapids, MI: Baker Book House, 1973), 55, 83.

9. 1 Cor. 15:7; Wilhelm Schneemelcher, ed., *New Testament Apocrypha*, 2 vols. (Philadelphia: Westminster Press, 1963), 1:165.

10. Roman Catholics and others teach a form of this concept: that the real presence of Christ enters in the Eucharist. They believe the risen Lord appeared during early Christian meals and returns during their sacred meal.

11. David O. McKay, "The Lord's Sacrament," *Instructor*, September 1963, 306.

Chapter 6

Doing the Works of God

The Gospels refer to the miracles of Jesus as "mighty works" and "signs" (Matt. 11:20; 14:2; Mark 6:2, 5, 14; 16:17, 20; Luke 19:37; John 20:30); but Jesus himself called them "the works of God" (John 9:3). The key to understanding why he does them—his one dominant purpose, was to fulfill the Father's will, or as Jesus himself said, "that the Father may be glorified in the Son" (John 14:13). He did not regard any of his works as his own; rather, they were the Father's works. They therefore became evidences of the Father's pleasure in the Son and witnesses to Christ's divine claims. The New Testament records thirty-five specific miracles that Jesus performed, which can be summarized under three convenient headings: (1) healings, (2) control over nature, and (3) raising the dead.

In addition to the twenty-three specific healings identified in the Gospels—including six exorcisms—there are general references to the many healings of Jesus. The synoptic writers record:

> They brought unto him all sick people that were taken
> with divers diseases and torments, and those which were pos-
> sessed with devils, and those which were lunatick [possibly

meaning epileptic?], and those that had the palsy; and he healed them. (Matt. 4:24)

And great multitudes came unto him, having with them those that were lame, blind, dumb, maimed, and many others, and cast them down at Jesus' feet; and he healed them. (Matt. 15:30)

He departed from Galilee, and came into the coasts of Judea beyond Jordan;
And great multitudes followed him; and he healed them there. (Matt. 19:1–2)

And whithersoever he entered, into villages, or cities, or [the] country, they laid the sick in the streets, and besought him that they might touch if it were but the border of his garment: and as many as touched him were made whole. (Mark 6:56; cf. Matt. 14:35–36)

All they that had any sick with divers diseases brought them unto him; and he laid his hands on every one of them, and healed them. (Luke 4:40)

And a great multitude of people [came] out of all Judea and Jerusalem, and from the sea coast of Tyre and Sidon, which came to hear him, and to be healed of their diseases. . . .

And [Jesus] healed them all. (Luke 6:17, 19; cf. Matt. 8:16)

When Jesus healed people physically, he also removed inferiority complexes, improved their self-image, and restored their social standing in the community, particularly those with chronic maladies such as lepers, discharges, and the blind. Prior to being healed, these people had often been shunned for years, looked down upon and stigmatized as "sinners." Thus, when

"Making a blind man "whole"–physically, emotionally, socially, and spiritually

Jesus healed them, their personality and spiritual life also changed. He often said that he had made them "whole." In other words he healed them physically, emotionally, socially, and spiritually (John 5:1-15; John 9; Mark 5:25-34; esp. Luke 17:11-19).

The citations above demonstrate Jesus' empathy for the suffering and his willingness to answer requests. The miracles show the extent of his great love and compassion for people. No prophet before or after Jesus has ever made so many people "whole." Thus, it was natural that the people would say of Jesus midway through his ministry: "A great prophet is risen up among us," and "One of the old prophets is risen again" (Luke 7:16; 9:18-19; Matt. 16:13-14; Mark 8:27-28). After all, Moses, Elijah, Elisha, Daniel, and other great Old Testament prophets all performed miracles. Consequently, many identified Jesus as being in this same tradition.

However, some noticed that Jesus was in fact different from all the Old Testament prophets. John noted: "Many of the people believed on him, and said, When Christ cometh, will he do more miracles than these which this man hath done? . . . Of a truth this is the Prophet . . . This is the Christ. . . . Never man spake like this man" (John 7:31, 40-41, 46).

Some people, for example, observed that while the prophet Elijah had miraculously provided food for a widow and her son for feeding him (1 Kgs. 17:8-16; Matt. 14:15-21), Jesus, using two small fish and five loaves, fed a crowd of about 15,000 men, women, and children, and had more food left over than he had started with. They knew that Elisha the prophet had made an iron axe float on the River Jordan, but Jesus walked "thirty furlongs" (over three miles) across the Sea of Galilee (John 6:19; 2 Kgs. 6:5-7). These miracles markedly surpassed those of the ancient prophets.

The scriptures record ten miracles in which Jesus controlled the forces of nature. He turned water to wine. He called up two separate draughts of fishes. He stilled a tempest. He multiplied food to feed one multitude of five thousand men (accompanied by women and children) and another of four thousand. He walked on water and Peter's faith in Jesus temporarily also sustained him on water. He provided tax money in a fish caught apparently at random. He cursed a fig tree, withering it overnight (John 2:1–11; Luke 5:1–10; John 21:6; Matt. 8:23–27; 14:13–21; 15:32–39; Luke 9:13–17; Mark 8:1–9; Matt. 14:25; 17:24–27; 21:18–22).

However, his first and greatest miracle over nature was done even before he came to earth. As the premortal Creator, he organized chaotic materials into an earth and pronounced it "very good" for humankind. Thus, while the prophet Moses had performed many great miracles over nature in the Old Testament, some disciples also knew that Jesus Christ was involved in those very miracles and that, "All things were made by him. . . . The world was made by him" (Gen. 1:31; John 1:3, 10).

A number of people also observed a difference from the Old Testament prophets in his raising of the dead. Elijah had revived the dead son of the widow of Zarephath, and Elisha had raised up the dead son of the Shunammite woman—essentially once in their lives (1 Kgs. 17:17–24; 2 Kgs. 4:32–37). But Jesus in his short three-year ministry raised four individuals from the dead. Furthermore, these four accounts progressed in dramatic power. When Jesus raised Jairus's daughter, who had died while Jesus was en route to her, he said: "The maid is not dead, but sleepeth" (Matt. 9:18–26). He then restored her to life, even though the mourners had already begun wailing. At Nain, Jesus stopped a funeral procession which was actually on its way to the cemetery, lifted the widow's son from the bier, and presented him alive and well to his widowed mother (Luke 7:11–15). At Bethany, Jesus raised Lazarus from the dead after he had been in the tomb four days. The fame of this miracle was

"*I am* the resurrection. . . . Lazarus, come forth" (John 11)

.

such that "many of the Jews . . . believed on him" (John 11:1-45).

When Jesus made his final Sunday entry into Jerusalem during the Passover, Jerusalem's normal population of 25,000 had increased to over 150,000, many of them Jewish pilgrims who lived outside Palestine.[1] Matthew observed: "And when he [Jesus] was come into Jerusalem, all the city was moved, saying, Who is this?" The multitude was deafening in their praise. Concerned about a riot, the Pharisees pushed through the crowd and demanded, "Master, rebuke thy disciples." Jesus replied, "I tell you that, If these should hold their peace, the stones would immediately cry out" who I am (Matt. 21:10; Luke 19:37-40).

On Tuesday the religious leaders asked four final questions of Jesus, and he asked one of them: "What think ye of Christ? Whose son is he?" (Mark 11:27-33; 12:1-17; Matt. 22:23-46). Their response was to stage a trial of dubious legality with the connivance of the Roman authorities, convict him, and crucify him on Friday. On Easter morning, they had Jesus' own answer to his question—the supreme miracle of all time. He was not just restoring life to a corpse, awesome though this achievement is. All three of those called back from the dead—the young maiden, the widow's son, and Lazarus—would again face death at some point in their future. But Jesus did not simply continue a temporarily interrupted mortal life. Rather, he *conquered* death so that his flesh and bone became immortal, glorified, no longer subject to death (Matt. 28; Mark 16; Luke 24; John 20).

Nor did Jesus stop there. He underscored his victory over the grave by resurrecting an unspecified number of people who "came out of the graves after his resurrection, and went into the holy city [Jerusalem], and appeared unto many" (Matt. 27:50-53). In short, Jesus not only did the same type of miracles as the Old Testament prophets, but he performed them more frequently and more dramatically. For many, the ability of Jesus to restore life in this supreme progression demonstrated conclusively who he was.

Why is it that Jesus can do so many "works of God" but that we as his disciples are less confident? The answer, I believe, has something to do with our degree of faith or trust in the Father and with our own degree of goodness. For instance, when Jesus told his disciples that he would feed a multitude of 15,000 with two small fish and five loaves, they simply did not believe he could do it, even though they had seen Jesus perform a number of previous miracles. Disappointed in their lack of faith, Jesus was slow to intervene the next time they had a request. Instead, he watched them from a mountain top while they were "toiling in rowing" in a storm for nearly twelve hours (from the first to the fourth watch) before he intervened. He rescued them only after a trial of their faith because they needed to have stronger faith (Mark 6:46-51). Jesus also told his disciples on another occasion that they failed to heal a man "because of your unbelief," and because they needed to conjoin "prayer and fasting," indicating their need for a closer relationship with God and more humility (Matt. 17:20-21).

Jesus received quick responses from the Father because the characteristics of the Father were in him. Moreover, his faith was strong because of his previous experiences with the Father. The Father trusted him. He knew Jesus did not need to have his faith tested in what he requested. Therefore, the Father granted "whatsoever he saith" immediately, excepting only the crucial point of the atonement where Jesus' desire to avoid that agony could not be granted. But even there, Jesus manifested his faith in his Father by submitting freely to his will. Jesus promises the same to all his disciples:

> Have faith in God.
> For verily I say unto you, That whosoever shall . . .

"He will swallow up death in victory; and the . . . . dead . . .
shall live, together with . . . [their] body shall they arise"
(Isa. 25:8; 26:19)

believe that those things which he saith shall come to pass; he shall have whatsoever he saith.

Therefore I say unto you, What things soever ye desire, when ye pray, believe that ye receive them, and ye shall have them. (Mark 11:22–24; cf. 1 John 5:14–15)

And again:

Ask, and it shall be given you; seek, and ye shall find; knock, and it shall be opened unto you. . . .

What man is there of you, whom if his son ask bread, will he give him a stone?

Or if he asks a fish, will he give him a serpent?

If ye then, being evil, know how to give good gifts unto your children, how much more shall your Father which is in heaven give good things to them that ask him? (Matt. 7:7–11)

Jesus and the Father gave fish and bread freely, never stones or serpents. How and when they bless us, however, is often determined by the degree of our faith and the extent to which the characteristics of Jesus and the Father abide in us.

As followers of Jesus, it is important for us to pay close attention to his words and actions. We observe that during his formative years that "Jesus increased . . . in favour with God" (Luke 2:52). This "increase" undoubtedly included Jesus' careful study of the scriptures, for by the beginning of his ministry he knew them well (Luke 4:3–12). Jesus said of the Father, "I know him" and "the Father knoweth me" (John 8:55; 10:15). After his baptism, "the Holy Ghost" or First Comforter, "descended . . . upon him," and then "a voice came from heaven, which said, Thou art my beloved Son; in thee I am well pleased" (Luke 3:21–22). This event was the sign that the Father, his Second Comforter, abode in him and was available to him in his ministry. Jesus promises the same to all his disciples.

He that believeth on me, the works that I do shall he do also; and greater works than these shall he do; because I go unto my Father.

And whatsoever ye shall ask in my name, that will I do, that the Father may be glorified in the Son.

If ye shall ask any thing in my name, I will do it. . . .

And will manifest myself to him. . . . If a man *love me*, he will keep my words: and my Father will love him, and we will come unto him, and make our abode with him . . . He that abideth in me, and I in him, the same bringeth forth much fruit . . . *If ye abide in me, and my words abide in you, ye shall ask what ye will, and it shall be done unto you.* (John 14:12–14, 21–23; 15:5, 7; emphasis mine)

Several of the promises in these scriptural passages were repeated to me over thirty years ago. I was teaching high school and some college students at the LDS Church College of New Zealand when, in May 1970, I was hired to be director of an LDS Institute of Religion in southern California. Feeling inadequate, I prayed one night to be made equal to the task. My wife Kathy was asleep in bed next to me, but I was very much awake as I humbly asked God to reveal my weaknesses. I expected an answer from the Holy Ghost because his Spirit was strong, but he did not answer me. Instead, an unseen presence entered my doorway that was so much stronger than the Holy Spirit that tears instantly sprang to my eyes and fell onto my cheeks. I strongly sensed that it was the Lord Jesus Christ. I thought that I would see him, but I did not. His presence moved to the foot of my bed and I asked him my question. Instantly, one of my weaknesses entered my mind, and then another. I had not been aware of this second one, and losing my focus, began thinking about it. The divine presence started to move toward the door. I immediately said, "I accept it," and he returned to the foot of my bed. Then a third weakness entered my mind.

He now moved to my side of the bed; and as he did so, his question came into my mind, asking: "What else do you want to know"?

I replied, "To understand the atonement."[2]

He then asked, "What else?"

I said somewhat hesitantly, "To see you one day."

His answer was: "Love me and you will." The first two words, "love me," were uttered in an audible whisper. I heard it in my mind and with my ears simultaneously. The last three, "and you will," were spoken in normal verbal speech. The Lord then left my room. Jesus was quoting from John 14:23 (cited above), but I did not know the Bible well enough at the time to recognize the source. I remained awake all night, marveling over this experience. It was definitely not a dream. In the morning, I reverently shared it with my wife.

The Lord's further unsolicited gift to me was that, for the seven months that remained in the year, I felt His loving presence powerfully with me every day. It gave new meaning to the term "grace" and "graciousness." His gifts made me confident in my assignment as I began teaching Institute of Religion classes in September.

Jesus Christ is the model of what a person can do after receiving the Second Comforter, "For in him [Jesus] dwelleth all the fullness of the Godhead bodily" (Col. 2:9). What Jesus does is what we can potentially do. With the Godhead (Father, Son, and Holy Ghost) indwelling in us, Jesus will "manifest" himself in our lives. We too can ask to see and hear things about our ministry. We too can do the "works of God," "bringing forth much fruit." This is a mighty gift from God. It is the gift of Eternal Life; the gift of Jesus himself to us. He offers the First and Second Comforters to all, inviting all to the great supper. He will honor the covenant of anyone willing to accept his name in the rite of baptism and apply the atonement. As leader of the Church, Peter plainly preached how to apply the atonement in one's life. He counseled all who had faith in Christ to: "Be partakers of the divine nature" of Jesus Christ and escape the "corruption that is in the world" and by exercising

all diligence, add to your faith virtue; and to virtue knowledge;

And to knowledge temperance; and to temperance patience; and to patience godliness;

And to godliness brotherly kindness; and to brotherly kindness charity.

For if these things be in you, and abound, they make you that ye shall neither be barren nor unfruitful in the knowledge of our Lord Jesus Christ. . . .

Give diligence to make your calling and election sure: for if ye do these things, ye shall never fall. . . .

And the day star [the Second Comforter, will] arise in your hearts. (2 Pet. 1:4-8, 10, 19. Compare v. 19 with Rev. 2:28; 22:16)

Nothing more is required to dwell with the Godhead, here or hereafter. It is our "diligence" and the influence of the enabling grace of Christ—"the day star"—that empowers us to employ the nine qualities of the atonement to "overcome the world" (John 16:33). The more we "put on Christ"and "Christ be in [us]," the more good we can do for others (Rom. 8:10; 13:14). For when the Father and Son "make [their] abode with [us]," an experience known as receiving the Second Comforter, they respond to our requests sooner and more often. Thus, "the Father [and Son] may be glorified" by us also (John 14:13). This is the key for the growth and influence of Christianity.

Of all the Christmas carols that we sing during that holiday season, the one that I believe best captures Jesus Christ is, "Silent night! Holy night! / All is calm, all is bright." How bright was it that night? There have been many lights seen in this world, especially during our own electronic and nuclear

Out of Bethlehem came the brightest light

age, but the brightest came out of Bethlehem. On that night, space was turned upside down, for as Mary and Joseph cradled the child, they knew they were looking down at "the Son of the Highest," the "Son of Man." The truest image of "Man of Holiness"—the son of Man of Holiness—began to be revealed on Christmas Day.[3]

෫෦෬

Notes

1. We can calculate this increase by the number of Pascal lambs that were sacrificed on this holiday during Christ's era; Joachim Jeremias, *Jerusalem in the Time of Jesus* (Philadelphia: Fortress Press, 1969), 27, 58-84.

2. Shortly after this experience I discovered John 12. See Chapter 5, "The Meaning of Atonement."

3. Luke 1:32; Mark 2:28; Jesus uses the term "Son of Man" more than eighty times in the Gospels. For "Man of Holiness," see Gen. 2:23; Moses 6:57.

Chapter 7

Finding Jesus in Jail

The most tragic words ever written about Jesus were that "he came unto his own, and his own received him not" (John 1:11). At Bethlehem, there was no room for him in the inn at his birth; at Nazareth, there was no room for him among his townspeople; at Jerusalem, there was no room for him to teach in the temple or even a tomb for him where he died. Jesus knew well feelings of rejection, loneliness, homelessness, and abandonment. He knew what it was like to be forced to move on, to be arrested, chained, mocked, and physically abused by prison guards. He knew what it was like to be paraded before the curious, to appear before judges and magistrates, and to receive a sentence even of death.

Thus, Jesus is uniquely qualified to succor those who are in the jails and prisons of the world. During his mortal ministry, he devoted much of his time to sinners, the sick, the poor and despised, and he has not changed his ways. Jesus does not appear only in sanctuaries and temples as some may believe. He also walks the halls and visits the cells of the world's prisons. I have found him and the signs of his healing ministry in the Salt Lake County Jail.

Most inmates in jail have lost everything. Whatever material goods they possessed before their incarceration are usually lost once they enter the jail. They lose their employment. Unable to make payments, they soon lose their car, house, clothes, furniture, and other belongings. Often their spouse or lover forsakes them, which usually means they may not see or correspond with their children very often—sometimes never. Friends shun them. Moreover, they are housed in very small living spaces with limited movement and few privileges. Their life is at a stand-still, and virtually all aspects of their lives are no longer in their control. Depression is a common problem, and many sleep virtually around the clock as an escape. Their anxiety level is usually high because they are waiting to be sentenced. Their future is unknown. After they serve their sentences, some find "yellow ribbons." Others find closed doors. This generalized thumbnail sketch is rather typical of the inmates that I observed during my thirteen-year ministry as a chaplain and LDS Institute director at the Salt Lake County jail.

Can any good result in such circumstances? The answer depends on how the inmate chooses to handle his or her jail experience. I often suggest they read the scriptural account of Joseph of Egypt when he was incarcerated and embrace his attitude (Gen. 37–45). At age seventeen, Joseph was sold into slavery by his own brothers, becoming a slave in Potiphar's house. Piling injustice upon injustice, his diligent service was "rewarded" by the efforts of his master's wife to seduce him. When he rejected her advances, she claimed that Joseph had tried to rape her. As a foreigner and a slave, he was fortunate to have escaped the death penalty. He served about ten years in prison. Perhaps for a time Joseph felt sorry for himself. After all, he was a stranger in a strange land, confronted with a language, culture, and religion that was entirely unlike his own. His feelings toward his brothers were probably very bitter. Perhaps he questioned God's existence, and certainly his youthful faith was sorely tested. Why had God not intervened to save him, either from his brothers' envy, from slavery, or from prison, especially since he was innocent?

Joseph had every reason to give up, but he did not. Instead, he became a church of one. He did not have the scriptures or weekly services to strengthen him, but he did have the memories of his father, Jacob, the teachings about God that had come down to him in his family, and his own intense faith and prayers. Rather than despairing, Joseph placed his future in God's hands and eventually became the number two man in all of Egypt under Pharaoh, who gave him extensive authority. When his brothers came to Egypt years later in desperate need of food, he did not seek revenge but reconciliation. He treated them far better than they expected.

Typically inmates have received much counseling and advice from parents, school counselors, psychologists, and even psychiatrists in their young lives. And typically, this advice didn't "take," or the inmate would not be incarcerated. Furthermore, although genuine miscarriages of justice do occur, I think it is far more likely that the American justice system operates quite leniently and that most people in jail have good reason for being there. Yet Jesus, during his mortal ministry healed people emotionally, socially, spiritually, and physically, usually meeting with them only once.

As a chaplain, I often invited the Great Physician to intervene in my ministry and to honor his promise to his disciples: "He that believeth on me, the works that I do shall he do also" (John 14:12-14). Before I would begin a counseling session with an inmate, I would pray—simply asking Jesus Christ that the words spoken would be his words and that the action taken would make the counselee whole. From time to time, I have received letters from inmates whose experience testifies to Christ's power to heal through prison bars. For example, after I counseled one inmate, he wrote: "As you talked with me the spirit was so strong with us that I came close to tears several times. Crying is something very difficult for me to do, but I welcome it when it happens. Your words seemed as though they were coming directly from the Lord, through you. It was like you were talking to my spirit which recognized the voice. . . . When I heard what you told me, I believed it. For the first time in my ordeal, I had hope. I went back to my cell and cried harder than I had in a long, long time, because of my experience."

I gave over a thousand priesthood blessings to inmates in the Salt Lake County Jail during my thirteen-year ministry. One inmate would tell another, who would then request a blessing from me. Their culture or religious background seemed irrelevant to them and certainly was to me. To them, blessings were simply part of the jail experience. They asked for a blessing because it gave them hope. I feel that such blessings were the most productive part of my ministry in jail. I always prefaced these blessings with my personal prayer that the Lord's will would be done. Sometimes the Spirit constrained me as I spoke; but more frequently, I felt a spirit of grace abounding. On these occasions, I was bold rather than timid in what I said. The incomparable Jesus was true to his promise, honoring the faith that was present. I feel that it is appropriate to share some of these testimonies of Christ's transforming love.

I counseled a young woman who bitterly hated her father. She came to transfer this hatred to all men, including God. I talked with her for forty-five minutes without progress. Finally I asked if I could give her a blessing. To my surprise, she agreed. Laying my hands upon her head, I said simply, "Your Father in Heaven loves you." I could not speak another word. The Spirit descended upon us both so powerfully that utterance simply wasn't possible. After more than two minutes, I closed the blessing. Afterward I asked, "Do you know that your Heavenly Father loves you?" Weeping with emotion, she said, "Yes." Two minutes of feeling the Spirit accomplished what forty-five minutes of counseling had failed to do.

I counseled another young woman who had been sexually abused and raped by her father. She was struggling with feelings of great bitterness and hatred for him. She wanted to forgive him, had prayed to forgive him, and had talked through the process of forgiving him in her mind. Nevertheless, bitterness remained deep in her heart. She asked me for a blessing to remove the hate.

As I spoke the blessing, the words that came were that she needed to ask her father's forgiveness for the hatred and bitterness she was feeling. She was irate with me, saying: "I forgive him? He sexually abused me for years and has never even admitted what he did to me." I certainly understood her surprise, but I simply told her that the idea had not been mine. I asked her to exercise her faith and to contact her father. Several weeks went by while she continued to struggle. Finally, she was able to ask for a meeting. She poured out her pain to him and asked him to forgive her for her hatred toward him. A miracle occurred. His walls of denial collapsed. In turn, he asked her to forgive him for the horrible things he had done to her during her teenage years. She was astounded and, from that moment on, began healing.

A thirty-one-year-old inmate was sentenced to life without parole for the first-degree murder of his business partner. He was an elder in the LDS church and believed that, for him, there was "no forgiveness in this world or in the world to come." He wanted to see me about this problem. On the way to visit him, I asked the Lord how I could give him hope. The following sequence of ideas entered my mind: (1) The mental anguish that he was suffering would soon end. (2) He should resolve to do all the good he could for others for the rest of his life in prison. (3) In the next world, he would need to receive his partner's forgiveness. (4) Then, and only then, I heard in my mind from the Savior: "He will come before me and I will pardon him." These words gave the inmate hope. This incident reveals to me just how far the Lord is willing to go to provide hope and to save a soul.

Another inmate who had murdered his wife told me that he hurt physically, all over his body, as if his mental anguish was literally causing the severe bodily pain. He said that he pled with the Lord to take away the pain for one-half hour each day. This prayer was granted. "During the last two months," he said, "I live for that brief reprieve from the pain." Apparently, this man was the recipient of the Lord's promise: "I will not leave you comfortless: I will come to you" (John 14:18). Such is the mercy of Jesus Christ.

Jenny (a pseudonym), a young woman from Thailand, approached me one day in the jail and said in broken English: "A nice looking women in a gold dress with long black hair and fingernails keeps appearing and making threats to me." These appearances had been occurring for about three years, both in dreams and also while Jenny was awake. Frightened, she asked me for a blessing. I had not spoken for more than five seconds when her whole body jolted dramatically. She trembled, groaned, and twisted her head about, seeking to shake my hands away. The woman-spirit was actually inside her body. In the name of Jesus Christ, I ordered the woman to leave her and her cell. Afterward, Jenny said she was weak and dizzy. She also said that she felt something come out of her, followed by a sensation of relief and pleasure like "snowflakes hitting her skin on her whole body." It was a lovely way of expressing what the Spirit felt like. I told her that I would visit her the next day but that she should pray, thank the Lord for this blessing, and occupy her mind by reading the scriptures until I returned.

The following morning, she greeted me with a radiant countenance. She reported that, before I arrived, she had again encountered the woman-spirit in the day room. This time the woman's eyes were filled with anger, a new development. She was angry that Jenny had talked with me and angry about the blessing. The spirit-woman also acknowledged to Jenny that she was not allowed to enter Jenny's cell. In her broken English, Jenny said, "because it was like many snowflakes were coming down from each wall. This kept her out." I shall certainly not forget the contrast between the fear on Jenny's face on the day of the blessing compared with her peaceful and happy countenance the next morning.

After working with sex offenders for a number of years, I made a rather startling observation regarding some of these offenders. God's Spirit was powerfully with them in their lives, even though they had recently been jailed. They neither understood the process of repentance nor had they had time to repent of these horrible deeds. I asked the Lord about this apparent contradiction, since it was both confusing and baffling to me. In my several prayers, the following scripture came to mind:

> And whoso shall receive one such little child in my name receiveth me.
> But whoso shall offend one of these little ones which believe in me, it were better for him that a millstone were hanged about his neck, and that he were drowned in the depth of the sea. (Matt. 18:5–6)

The idea impressed upon my mind was that, if an adult takes away the innocence of a child, the adult will have to pay for his own sins and for the sins of the child that he sexually offends. Sexually violated children usually have several social problems, especially as teenagers. Some of them then go on to sexually abuse other children or their own children as adults. Under these circumstances, it seems that God does not hold them totally responsible for their sexual crimes but rather holds the originator of these horrible deeds more accountable. In each case the Lord's Spirit was with these men and women, not because he had forgiven them, but to compensate for the sins of their fathers and, in some cases, grandfathers, or other adult relatives or friends. God in his love and graciousness was succoring those who were the recipients of these evil "traditions of the fathers."

One inmate from a prominent religious family whom I had counseled for over a year told me that his grandfather had sexually abused his father, who had sexually abused him, and that he in turn had sexually abused his own son. He broke down in tears when I told him what I had learned in my prayers. He said, "There are members of my extended family who do not want me to make this family secret known, but I promise you that this evil tradition will be reported and will end with me." The sins of the fathers may be visited upon the children unto the third and fourth generation, but it is the father or originator of these evil deeds whom God holds responsible for these actions. When a child's innocence is taken away by an adult, he is often psychologically damaged, making his subsequent behavior abnormal. When he grows up and abuses another child the court system punishes his behavior, as it should, but God looks upon him as less culpable, even though his actions are evil, because he too is a victim. Although Christ's grace and mercy do not excuse their sins, it is a powerful message of hope about the possibility and the promise of repentance and forgiveness.

While Jesus is mainly interested in holiness, his second focus is clearly compassion. This we see in the four Gospels, not in so many episodes of giving money or material goods—although Jesus and his apostles did give money "to the poor" (John 12:5)—but in his many more numerous episodes of healing, forgiving, and accepting others. With Jesus, there is no "them" and "us," only "us." The word compassion means "with passion," or how we feel toward others unlike ourselves. One of my experiences of "finding Jesus in jail" was for my own benefit.

In counseling many homosexuals and lesbians during my ministry, I usually found them to be honest and forthright regarding their sexuality. They informed me that they discovered their sexual orientation, usually at an early age. Typically they did not choose it. One memorable and flamboyant individual related his whole painful life story. He detailed his pain and persecution from age three. He reported that he felt like Jesus because of the persecution he had received all his life for his homosexual tendencies and behavior. However, unlike Jesus, he did not return good for evil but had retaliated against his tormentors, which often brought him to jail. Seeking revenge on his many persecutors had only resulted in a long rap sheet. He was now facing serious time in prison. After several counseling sessions, he repented and resolved that he would indeed turn the other cheek when persecuted, beginning now while he was incarcerated. The inmate benefited from the counseling sessions, but I believe that I was the greater benefactor. I had heard the painful stories of other inmates over the years; but when this person began to share his burden with me, the Spirit enveloped me and I felt his pain down inside the depths of my soul, as if it were my own life experience. God wanted me to know what it was really like. I experienced with passion this man's burden, and it changed me forever. This experience softened my attitude, and I am grateful to the Lord for such a gift.

Several months later I viewed a film centered on a biblical theme: "The Lord seeth not as man seeth; for man looketh on the outward appearance, but the Lord looketh on the heart" (1 Sam. 16:7). In this movie, *Shallow Hal*, a guidance counselor placed a hex upon the film's star. Consequently, when he observed a nice woman with a good heart, he also saw the woman as outwardly slender and beautiful, even if she was excessively obese. When he began dating such women, his friends tried to get him to see what they saw (an ugly and extremely fat woman), but to no avail. The film was billed as light comedy, but it soon became apparent to me that it was a severe indictment upon society and the way we think about and ignore obese persons. I found myself feeling the collective pain, suffering, humiliation, and rejection experienced by all social outcasts. I cried as I thought about the attitude I had grown up with toward such people and how society as a whole treated them. I left the theater somber and reflecting upon my experience that went beyond the screen.

Several months later I was watching the news about the revenge killings that were occurring in the Middle East. I began to feel the collective grief of those Israeli and Palestinian families. It came to me in waves, and I did not like the experience. Two weeks later, I experienced a fourth and then the following week a fifth and a sixth experience. The sixth one was deeper, broader, and lasted much longer than the other ones. It occurred in the afternoon. I simply lost emotional control and could not be consoled. By bedtime my emotions were under control; but my mind was riveted upon the feelings, images, and burdens carried by other people. As I continued to ponder and struggle with these traumatic feelings, the message of this tutorial came from the Lord Jesus Christ. He brought to my remembrance one by one each of these six experiences. He connected the dots for me—something I had failed to see—perhaps because the six experiences had occurred over the period of nearly a year. He then said to me, "You have diligently prayed to know what I am like. That is what I am like."

Finally I understood. Jesus' heightened feelings of compassion did not begin in Gethsemane but culminated there in a blood-sweat. *All* his adult life he had a heightened sense of the pain, suffering, and burdens carried by other people. This is why he could never turn down requests. Because he had the power to heal people, he willed their wholeness. It was how he spent his time. It was who he was. He never turned anyone away. He was filled with such compassion that he simply could not say no. The requests of him at times were so demanding that his secondary mission of teaching compassion nearly over-

An angel "strengthening" Jesus in Gethsemane
(Luke 22:43)

whelmed his primary teaching mission—to reflect the Father's character to make people holy.

In Gethsemane and on the cross, Jesus felt the full measure of *responsibility* for the collective burdens of humanity. The Father wanted him to feel the full measure of human pain, suffering, and the collective burden of our sins because he would soon be responsible for judging all humankind. His experience was horrific and finally ended on the cross when "he cried with a loud voice"—"It is finished!" (Mark 15:37; John 19:30).

The Lord had given me a small bitter cup to drink that I might understand the way he is. It was sweet to have experienced a heightened sense of compassion for homosexuals, the obese, the grieving, children, and the elderly. I asked him to take away the bitter side of feeling the collective burdens of others. I simply could not deal with it. He heard my request and ended these experiences. I am grateful that the Lord indelibly stamped this degree of compassion upon my soul because it has unquestionably changed my attitude. The Lord knows that when a person has a proper attitude and then has an experience with an excessively obese person, a homosexual, someone grieving, or suffering in any other way, then what to say and how to act will flow from us naturally. The awkwardness is gone. We instinctively feel inclusiveness and acceptance. It is not necessary to think, "Now, let's see. What should be my response as a Christian in this situation? What did they teach me at church that I should do?"

All during the Lord's ministry, he sought to elevate the attitudes of his hearers. Jesus raised the Old Testament law of "love thy neighbor, and hate thine enemy" to the Golden Rule of "love your enemies, bless them that curse you, do good to them that hate you, and pray for them which despitefully use you, and persecute you" (Matt. 5:43-44). During the last week of his life, while administering the Last Supper, he again raised

the standard of what he expected from his disciples. First, he·
washed his apostles' feet and then said: "A new commandment
I give unto you, That ye love one another; as I have loved you."
What they did not know at that point was that his love included laying down his life for them. He continued: "[I command]
that ye also love one another. By this shall all men know that ye
are my disciples, if ye have love one to another" (John
13:34–35). In light of the Lord's heightened capacity for compassion and love toward us, it is obvious that his disciples then
and now fail to grasp the full meaning of his "new" commandment. The gospel net catches many different kinds of fish, as it
were. If Christian congregations today conscientiously applied
this higher expectation, the result would be far more love,
acceptance, and unity among us.

During my tutorial with the Lord, he made it clear that
he was not just "a man of sorrows, and acquainted with grief"
(Isa. 53:3) but also had experienced great joy at times during his
ministry. He simply felt the burdens of others more deeply and
experienced exquisite joy more deeply than humans are capable
of. For example, when he died on the cross, Jesus, having fully
gained his Father's trust immediately received the keys to resurrect, judge, and assign to the appropriate kingdom every human
who ever had lived or who ever would live on the earth. This
gave him great joy. The moment he died, he was instantly in the
world of spirits. There, according to Joseph F. Smith's vision of
the redemption of the dead, he received an altogether different
reception than the near-total rejection that he experienced at his
death. Waiting to welcome and adore him was a vast multitude
of the righteous dead from Adam down to his own time. They
worshipped him. They sang hymns of praise to him. He immediately began teaching them how to resurrect themselves from
the dead and assigned them to enter into the celestial city of
God. This experience gave the Lord exquisite joy, a joy as exquisite as his suffering had been bitter. After his resurrection on

Easter morning, myriads of these spirits also resurrected from their graves from all over the earth (D&C 138; Matt. 27:52–53).

It is the Lord's heightened compassion for the burdens of others and his heightened sense of joy for others that cause him to work in the trenches with human beings. He knows that, by influencing them to change their attitudes, he can lift their burden of sin and bring joy into their hearts here and hereafter in the city of God. He understands perfectly why he walks the halls and visits the cells of the jails and prisons of this world.

Perhaps the greatest evidence of Jesus in jail is the many inmates who have informed me that their troubles seem smaller because their lives are now "swallowed up in Christ" (Mosiah 16:8). They are in company with Jesus rather than being isolated in their cells. Their many struggles and difficult lives have driven them to seek "the mind of Christ" (1 Cor. 2:16). In their humility, they meditate, pray, and read the Bible daily. Many have shared with me their heartfelt yearnings of wishing they had found God early in life, had been taken to church by their parents, had stayed in school, had avoided drugs and alcohol, had behaved kindly rather than engaging in violent behavior. But they are not fixated on these negative parts of their past. Despite their history of poor decision making and the habits that have resulted from them, the Lord does not forsake them:

> I am the true vine, and my Father is the husbandman . . .
> Every branch that beareth fruit, *he purgeth it, that it may bring forth more fruit.* . . .
> I am the vine, ye are the branches: He that abideth in me, and I in him, the same bringeth forth much fruit: for without me ye can do nothing. (John 15:1–2, 5; emphasis mine)

Jesus Christ is truly a husbandman. He designed the Garden of Eden and the Garden in the midst of the heavenly city of God. In the Garden of Gethsemane, he trod "the wine-press alone" (Isa. 63:3). In the Garden Tomb, he appeared to Mary first as the risen Christ. How ironic that she supposed "him to be the gardener" (John 20:15), for indeed he is! As our gardener, he prunes and seeks to shape us to be all we can be. We often complain about these prunings, but we wouldn't amount to much without them. We want the crown without the cross. We prefer tailor-made trials, but he often sends us challenges that we don't like. Jesus didn't get to make his own cross, and neither do we; but we can take what God has given us in faith, as Jesus did. In doing so, we become a stronger and a more complete person. I feel in my soul the truth of the Psalmist's words:

> He maketh me to lie down in green[er] pastures: he lead-eth me beside the still waters.
> He restoreth my soul: he leadeth me in the paths of righteousness. (Ps. 23:2-3)

I even feel to say, "Lord, you carry me as 'I walk through the valley of the shadow of death' and my faith and hope are that 'I will dwell in the house of the Lord for ever'" (Ps. 23:4, 6).

I have witnessed friends and relatives turn their backs on inmates when they are in denial and refuse to acknowledge their problems. They give up, feeling a frustration that is all too understandable in human terms. But the Lord with the outstretched arm is patient. I have worked closely enough with many of these men and women to observe his persistent, continuing influence with them. It is humbling to witness.

Thus, early in my jail experience I learned to be less judgmental and more willing to be patient with inmates. I observed the same inmates entering and leaving the jail several times. They were actually making progress. They were returning for a lesser crime than their original charge or for a parole violation. I well remember working with one inmate for several years. He had experienced many difficulties in his youth. He was one of six siblings, all born of different fathers. His mother was blind and did not have much control over the children. By age twelve, he had run away from home numerous times and had been in a number of foster homes. By age seventeen, he had served considerable time in juvenile reform schools and had attempted suicide four times. The scars were visible on his arms and wrists.

When I met this inmate he was about thirty-eight years old, and he had spent most of his life in a lock-up facility. He had a number of habitual problems that were difficult for him to overcome. One by one we worked on them. He gained confidence in himself and began to really hope, for the first time in many years, that he could change. Upon his release, he was indeed a different person with an optimistic view toward his future. Then three months later, I discovered that he had again returned to jail. When I found and talked with him, he was embarrassed. He said he had disappointed God, himself, and me. Despairingly, he said, "I've given up thinking I can change." Having observed the master teacher, I simply put my arm around him and said, "We will start over again." He wept.

Jesus remembers what we often seem to forget: that to enter the kingdom of heaven, a person does not have to receive the gold, silver, or bronze metal, or to be one of the first million to cross the finish line, but we do have to endure to the end and finish the race. It is true that some will cross that finish line crawling on their hands and knees in the dirt. But that is better than not finishing, for all who finish, whether first or last, will hear the voice of the Good Shepherd say: "Well done, my good and faithful servant. . . . Enter into the joy of thy Lord" (Matt. 25:21, paraphrased).

⁘⁙

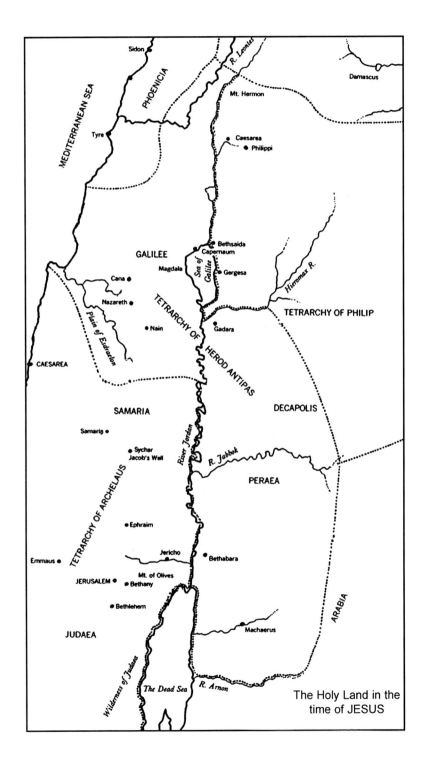

The Holy Land in the time of JESUS

Appendix

A Chronology of Jesus' Ministry

Place	Event	Reference
BIRTH AND PREPARATION		
Jerusalem	Annunciation of John to Zacharias.	Luke 1:5-25, 57-80
Nazareth	Annunciation of Christ to Mary.	Luke 1:26-38
Nazareth to Jerusalem	Mary visits Elizabeth.	Luke 1:39-55
Jerusalem to Nazareth	Mary returns three months pregnant.	Luke 1:56
Nazareth	Royal genealogy, King David to Joseph. Gabriel's instruction to Joseph.	Matt. 1:1-25
Nazareth to Bethlehem	Joseph enrolled to be taxed. Christ is born. Shepherds visit the Christ child.	Luke 2:1-20
Bethlehem to Jerusalem	Presented in the temple and blessed by Simeon and Anna.	Luke 2:21-38
Jerusalem to Bethlehem	The magi visit the Christ child.	Matt. 2:1-12
Flight to Egypt	Herod kills the innocents.	Matt. 2:13-18
Egypt to Nazareth		Luke 2:19-23
Nazareth to Jerusalem	Temple trip at age twelve.	Luke 2:41-51
Jerusalem to Nazareth	Jesus grows up in Nazareth, stays there until about age thirty.	Luke 2:52
Jordan River, near Peraea	Baptism of Jesus.	Matt. 3:1-17

Place	Event	Reference
Jordan River to Judean wilderness	Temptation of Jesus.	Luke 4:1-13
Judean wilderness then to Bethsaida	Jesus calls Andrew, John, Peter, Nathaniel and Philip as apostles.	John 1:35-51
Bethsaida to Cana	Attends a family wedding. Water turned into wine.	John 2:1-11
Cana to Capernaum	Household of Mary and kindred established.	John 2:12

GALILEAN MINISTRY

Place	Event	Reference
Capernaum to Jerusalem	First temple cleansing. Interview with Nicodemus.	John 2:13-22; 3:1-13
Jerusalem to Judean wilderness at Jordan	Disciples baptize at Jordan.	John 4:1-3
Judean wilderness to Samaria	Talks to a Samaritan woman at Jacob's well.	John 4:3-30, 40-42
Samaria to Sychar	Jesus spends several days preaching with good reception.	John 4:43-45
Sychar to Cana	Heals a nobleman's son without visiting him.	John 4:46-54
Cana to Nazareth Nazareth to Capernaum	First rejection at Nazareth.	Luke 4:16-30 Matt. 4:13-16
Capernaum to Bethsaida	Call reissued to Simon, Andrew, James, and John.	Luke 5:1-11
Bethsaida to Capernaum	Casts out several evil spirits. Heals Peter's mother-in law. Teaches in synagogues of Galilee.	Mark 1:21-45
Galilee to Capernaum	Heals an invalid and forgives his sins. Calls Matthew the tax collector as an apostle. Eats and socializes with sinners: the whole don't need a physician. Parable of new wine in old bottles.	Mark 2:1-22

Place	Event	Reference
Capernaum to Jerusalem	Heals man at pool of Bethesda on sabbath. Testifies of his forthcoming resurrection. The Father, John the Baptist, his works, and the scriptures all testify he is Christ.	John 5:1-47
Jerusalem to Galilee	Pharisees criticize disciples for plucking corn on the sabbath. Heals a man with a withered hand on sabbath. He ordains twelve apostles. Teaches Sermon on the Mount.	Mark 2:23-28; 3:1-7, 13-19; Matt. 5-7
On way to Capernaum	Heals centurion's servant without visiting him.	Luke 7:1-10
Capernaum to Nain	Jesus raises widow's son from the dead. John's disciples ask Jesus if he is the Christ; healings follow. At Simon the Pharisee's, a woman anoints Jesus; he forgives her sins.	Luke 7:11-17, 36-50; Matt. 11:2-19
Mission through Galilee	Jesus heals a man who is blind, dumb, and possessed by a devil. Art thou the Christ? Sign of Jonah given to the Pharisees. Parable of the sower.	Matt. 12:22-30, 38-40; 13:1-23
On route to Gadara by the sea	Jesus calms Sea of Galilee, heals man possessed by a "legion."	Mark 4:35-41; 5:1-20
Gadara to east Galilee	Woman healed by touching Jesus' robe. Daughter of Jairus raised from the dead.	Mark 5:21-43
Galilee to Nazareth	Second rejection at Nazareth.	Mark 6:1-6
Nazareth to Capernaum	Jesus sends the twelve on a mission.	Matt. 10:1-15

Place	Event	Reference
Castle of Machaerus?	John the Baptist killed by Herod Antipas, who feared killing John and fears Christ.	Mark 6:14-29
Near Sea of Galilee (at Capernaum?)	Apostles return from mission and report. Jesus feeds 5,000 and sends them away. Disciples go to Bethsaida by the sea while Jesus retreats to a mountain to pray and watches disciples battling a storm on the Galilee.	Mark 6:30-46
To Sea of Galilee	Jesus walks on the sea and saves disciples; Peter's attempt.	Mark 6:47-52; Matt. 14:28-33
Sea to Bethsaida to Capernaum	Big crowds follow Jesus. He gives his bread of life sermon. Many leave. Criticized for not following "the traditions of the elders."	John 6:22-69; Matt. 15:1-20

GENTILE AREA MINISTRY

Place	Event	Reference
Coasts of Phoenicia, at Tyre and Sidon	Jesus heals daughter of Syrophoencian woman.	Matt. 15:21-29
Phoenicia to Decapolis	Heals man of speech impediment. Feeds 4,000.	Mark 7:31-37; 8:1-9
By sea to Dalmanutha (near Magdala?)	Beware of the rules, regulations, and hypocrisy of the Pharisees.	Mark 8:10-13; Matt. 16:1-12
To Bethsaida by sea	Blind man healed.	Mark 8:22-26
Near Caesarea Philippi	Jesus asks: "Whom say ye that I am?" Peter bears witness. Jesus predicts his passion and resurrection. Find/lose your soul by following the Lord.	Matt. 16:13-23, 24-28
To Mount Hermon	Transfiguration of Jesus. Elijah, Moses, and the Father appear to Jesus.	Mark 9:2-10; Luke 9:28-36

Place	Event	Reference
From Mount Hermon	Jesus heals a man possessed by demons after disciples fail. (They needed to fast and pray.)	Mark 9:14-29
To Capernaum	Tribute money (all are subject to law). Dispute about who is the greatest (little children). Jesus outlines the process of forgiveness. Jesus tells the parable of the unforgiving servant, showing the importance of mercy. On doing God's work without his authority. Jesus calls the seventy and sends them on a mission. He is criticized for not going to Jerusalem for the Feast of Tabernacles. His "time is not yet."	Matt.17:24-27; 18:1-35; Luke 9:49-50; Mark 9:38-41; Luke 10:1-11,16; John 7:1-9
From Capernaum to Samaritan town	Messengers preparing the way are rejected. James and John want Jesus to curse the village; Jesus rebukes them. They go to another village.	Luke 9:51-56

JUDEAN MINISTRY

Place	Event	Reference
On to Jerusalem	Jesus secretly arrives. Great discussion at his not appearing as expected. He teaches at the temple, not at the feast: Doctrine of the Father (do it and "know"). Plotted murder made known. Sabbath breaking charges answered. Declares his Sonship in Godhead. Pharisees hearing the positive reactions of the people seek to destroy him. "Living waters" come from Christ. Different reactions.	John 7:10-53; 8:1-2

Place	Event	Reference
	Anger of the Pharisees. Spends the night at Mount of Olives.	
Returns to temple and teaches	Adulterous woman brought before him and forgiven (no accusers). "I am the light of the world." Bears record of his Godhead to Pharisees. People's difficulty in understanding the Lord (obviously intended). Sinner is not free, regardless of heritage. Devil is the father of murder. Pharisees accuse Jesus of having a devil. "Before Abraham was, I am"; Jesus leaves the temple (murder attempted). Return of the seventy. Jesus rejoices in their report. Parable of the Good Samaritan.	John 8:2-59; Luke 10:17-37
Jerusalem to Bethany	Martha serves food; Mary listens to Jesus.	Luke 10:38-42
In Judea?	Parable of the rich, selfish fool. Parable of the barren fig tree. Jesus heals man born blind. Jesus is the good shepherd who will die for the sheep.	Luke 12:13-21; 13:6-10; John 9: 1-41; 10:1-15
Jerusalem (last winter)	At Solomon's porch during the Feast of Dedication, the Jews demand to know if Jesus is the Christ. His life is threatened.	John 10:22-39

PERAEAN MINISTRY

Place	Event	Reference
Jerusalem to Peraea (near his baptism)	Woman healed of 18-year infirmity on sabbath. Parables of the mustard seed and leaven.	John 10:40-42; Luke 13:11-21

Place	Event	Reference
Through villages to Jerusalem	Jesus explains who is saved (those who know him). Pharisees warn Christ of Herod's threats. Jesus laments over Jerusalem, feeling their burdens. Invalid healed on Sabbath. Jesus preaches against status seeking. The great supper (those without time). Necessity of sacrifice. Answers Pharisees on why he eats and helps scribes and sinners (Luke 15): Parables of the 99 sheep and the 1, woman and the lost coin, and prodigal son. Teaches his disciples (Luke 16): How to be wise in their stewardship. Pharisees covet the Lord's following. Parable of the rich man and Lazarus (against exalting self).	Luke 13:22-35; 14-16
To Bethany	Jesus raises Lazarus from the dead.	John 11:1-46
At Jerusalem	Leading Jews fear Rome will take away their self-rule unless they remove Jesus. Caiaphas predicts that Jesus will die for the nation. Jewish council plots his death.	John 11:47-53, 55-57
Jesus leaves Bethany and goes to Ephraim		John 11:54
Ephraim to Jericho	Jesus heals ten lepers (one thanks him). Kingdom of God is within you. Parables of the unjust judge (on persistent prayer), Pharisee and the publican (who is saved and why).	Luke 17:11-21; 18:1-14

Place	Event	Reference
Jericho to coasts of Judea	Law of marriage and divorce (on motive). Receive kingdom of God as a little child. Rich ruler (necessary to sacrifice all). Apostles to judge the 12 tribes of Israel. Parable of laborers in the vineyard (God and the individual). Jesus foretells his death and "set his face to go to Jerusalem" (Matt. 20:18-19; cf. Luke 9:51). James and John ask for honors; Jesus teaches about being the servant of all.	Matt. 19:1-30; 20:1-28
Coasts of Judea to Jericho	Healing of Bartimaeus who was blind. Zacchaeus the publican converted. Parable of the pounds (using time and means).	Luke 18:35-43; 19:1-27
Jericho to Bethany to Jerusalem	Pharisees consider taking Lazarus's life. Mary anoints Jesus' feet for his burial.	John 12:1-11

PASSION WEEK AND RESURRECTION

Jerusalem & Bethany	Apostles get foal/ass's colt (Sun).	Mark 11:1-6
	Triumphal entry into Jerusalem (Sun).	Mark 11:7-11; Luke 19:37-40
	Jesus curses a fig tree (Mon).	Mark 11:12-14
	Jesus cleanses temple again (Tues).	Mark 11:15-19
	Jesus withers fig tree (Tues).	Mark 11:20-26
	Four challenges from apostate religious leaders (Tues): Temple delegation: "By what authority"? (Jesus gives parable of wicked steward.) Herodians: "Lawful to give tribute to Caesar"? Sadducees: "Whose wife in	Mark 11:27-33; 12:1-17; Matt. 22:23-46

Place	Event	Reference
	the resurrection?" Pharisees: "What is the greatest commandment?" Lord's question: What think ye of Christ"?	
	Final words to Pharisees (Tues).	Matt. 23:1-39
	Lord teaches about second coming (Tues):	Matt: 24-25
	Describes the conditions and events before his second advent. "Watch and be ready." Parable of ten virgins. Parable of the ten talents. Final judgment (sheep versus goats).	
	The Last Supper. Lord's instructions. (Wed-Thurs): Washes the disciples' feet. Introduces the sacrament. Jesus teaches: Remember him and duplicate his love which brings the Holy Spirit. Total love brings Second Comforter. "I am the vine, ye are the branches." Prays for disciples to be sanctified.	John 13-17
	Garden of Gethsemane (Thurs).	John 17
	Judas betrays him (Thurs).	John 18:1-11
	Jesus' trial (Fri).	John 18:12-40
	His crucifixion (Fri).	John 19
	Two days in the spirit world (Fri-Sat).	1 Pet. 3:18-21; 4:6
	His resurrection (early Sun. morning).	John 20:1-29; 21:1-24
	Forty-day ministry .	John 20:30-31; 21:25; Acts 1:1-4
	The ascension.	Acts 1:5-11

Subject Index

A

Adam, 128
Adam and Eve, 35, 73-74, 81
Alexander the Great, 68
Annas, 10
apostles, characters of, 66. See also individuals.
atonement, 61-62, 73-94

B

Barsabas, 86
Bassett, Arthur R., 4
Bathsheba, 13
beatitudes, 9-31, 35-37, 43, 52, 91
birth narratives, 94 note 7
Book of Mormon, 4-5
Buddhists, number of, 1

C

Caesar, 68, 70
Caiaphas (high priest), 10
Charlemagne, 68
children, and Jesus, 54-57, 71
Chinese traditional religion, number of members, 1
Christianity, diversity in denominations, 2
Christians, number of, 1
Christmas carols, 110

city of God, 73, 33-37, 128-30
compassion, of Jesus, 18, 99, 122, 124-27, 129
courage, of Jesus, 13

D

Daniel (Old Testament), 99
David (king), 13
death, 72. See also resurrection.
diligence, 27
disciples, relation to Jesus, 26, 30, 57-58
divorce, 60

E

Elijah (Old Testament), 62, 99-100
Elisha (Old Testament), 99-100
empathy, of Jesus, 48
enduring to the end, 131
equality under the law, 49-50
Essenes, 52
Eucharist (Roman Catholicism), 94 note 10
exaltation, 37

F

faith, 104-8
fall of humankind, 73-74
family, of Jesus, 26

143

Scripture Index

Pearl of Great Price

Moses 6:57 — 113
Moses 6:59 — 74

Grant H. Palmer (M.A., American history, Brigham Young University) is a three-time director of LDS Institutes of Religion in California and Utah, a former instructor at the Church College of New Zealand, and an LDS seminary teacher at two Utah locations. During the last thirteen years of a thirty-four year teaching career with the Church Educational System, he served as a chaplain and the LDS Institute director at the Salt Lake County Jail. He has been active in the Mormon History and John Whitmer Historical Associations and on the board of directors of the Salt Lake Legal Defenders Association. His extensive church service includes being a Temple Officiator, a High Councillor, and served in the High Priest Group, and as president of the Elders Quorum, Sunday School, and Young Men. He especially enjoyed teaching the gospel doctrine class and being the high priest instructor in his ward for many years. Now retired, his hobby is pigeon fancying and traveling. He has four children and ten grandchildren. He and his wife live in Sandy, Utah.

Also available from
GREG KOFFORD BOOKS

Perspectives on Mormon Theology Series

Brian D. Birch and Loyd Ericson, series editors

(forthcoming)

This series will feature multiple volumes published on particular theological topics of interest in Latter-day Saint thought. Volumes will be co-edited by leading scholars and graduate students whose interests and knowledge will ensure that the essays in each volume represent quality scholarship and acknowledge the diversity of thought found and expressed in Mormon theological studies. Topics for the first few volumes include: revelation, apostasy, atonement, scripture, and grace.

The *Perspectives on Mormon Theology* series will bring together the best of new and previously published essays on various theological subjects. Each volume will be both a valued resource for academics in Mormon Studies and an illuminating introduction to the broad and sophisticated approaches to Mormon theology.

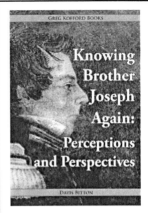

Knowing Brother Joseph Again: Perceptions and Perspectives

Davis Bitton

Paperback, ISBN: 978-1-58958-123-4

In 1996, Davis Bitton, one of Mormon history's preeminent and much-loved scholars, published a collection of essays on Joseph Smith under the title, *Images of the Prophet Joseph Smith*. A decade later, when the book went out of print, Davis began work on an updated version that would also include some of his other work on the Mormon prophet. The project was only partially finished when his health failed. He died on April 13, 2007, at age seventy-seven. With the aid of additional historians, *Knowing Brother Joseph Again: Perceptions and Perspectives* brings to completion Davis's final work—a testament to his own admiration of the Prophet Joseph Smith.

From Davis Bitton's introducton:

This is not a conventional biography of Joseph Smith, but its intended purpose should not be hard to grasp. That purpose is to trace how Joseph Smith has appeared from different points of view. It is the image of Joseph Smith rather than the man himself that I seek to delineate.

Even when we have cut through the rumor and misinformation that surround all public figures and agree on many details, differences of interpretation remain. We live in an age of relativism. What is beautiful for one is not for another, what is good and moral for one is not for another, and what is true for one is not for another. I shudder at the thought that my presentation here will lead to such soft relativism.

Yet the fact remains that different people saw Joseph Smith in different ways. Even his followers emphasized different facets at different times. From their own perspectives, different people saw him differently or focused on a different facet of his personality at different times. Inescapably, what they observed or found out about him was refracted through the lens of their own experience. Some of the different, flickering, not always compatible views are the subject of this book.

Excavating Mormon Pasts: The New Historiography of the Last Half Century

Newell G. Bringhurst and Lavina Fielding Anderson

Paperback, ISBN: 978-1-58958-115-9

Special Book Award - John Whitmer Historical Association

Mormonism was born less than 200 years ago, but in that short time it has developed into a dynamic world religious movement. With that growth has come the inevitable restructuring and reevaluation of its history and doctrine. Mormon and non-Mormon scholars alike have viewed Joseph Smith's religion as fertile soil for religious, historical and sociological studies. Many early attempts to either defend or defame the Church were at best sloppy and often dishonest. It has taken decades for Mormon scholarship to mature to its present state. The editors of this book have assembled 16 essays addressing the substantial number of published works in the field of Mormon studies from 1950 to the present. The contributors come from various segments of the Mormon tradition and fairly represent the broad intellectual spectrum of that tradition. Each essay focuses on a particular aspect of Mormonism (history, women's issues, polygamy, etc.), and each is careful to evenhandedly evaluate the strengths and weaknesses of the books under discussion. More importantly, each volume is placed in context with other, related works, giving the reader a panoramic view of contemporary research. Students of Mormonism will find this collection of historiographical essays an invaluable addition to their libraries.

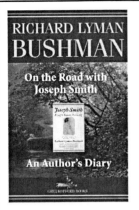

On the Road with Joseph Smith: An Author's Diary

Richard L. Bushman

Paperback, ISBN 978-1-58958-102-9

After living with Joseph Smith for seven years and delivering the final proofs of his landmark study, *Joseph Smith: Rough Stone Rolling* to Knopf in July 2005, biographer Richard Lyman Bushman went "on the road" for a year, crisscrossing the country from coast to coast, delivering addresses on Joseph Smith and attending book-signings for the new biography.

Bushman confesses to hope and humility as he awaits reviews. He frets at the polarization that dismissed the book as either too hard on Joseph Smith or too easy. He yields to a very human compulsion to check sales figures on Amazon. com, but partway through the process stepped back with the recognition, "The book seems to be cutting its own path now, just as [I] hoped."

For readers coming to grips with the ongoing puzzle of the Prophet and the troublesome dimensions of their own faith, Richard Bushman, openly but not insistently presents himself as a believer. "I believe enough to take Joseph Smith seriously," he says. He draws comfort both from what he calls his "mantra" ("Today I will be a follower of Jesus Christ") and also from ongoing engagement with the intellectual challenges of explaining Joseph Smith.

Praise for *On the Road With Joseph Smith*:

"The diary is possibly unparalleled—an author of a recent book candidly dissecting his experiences with both Mormon and non-Mormon audiences . . . certainly deserves wider distribution—in part because it shows a talented historian laying open his vulnerabilities, and also because it shows how much any historian lays on the line when he writes about Joseph Smith."
    -Dennis Lythgoe, *Deseret News*
"By turns humorous and poignant, this behind-the-scenes look at Richard Bushman's public and private ruminations about Joseph Smith reveals a great deal—not only about the inner life of one of our greatest scholars, but about Mormonism at the dawn of the 21st century."
    -Jana Riess, co-author of *Mormonism for Dummies*

The Brigham Young University Book of Mormon Symposium Series

Various Authors

Nine-volume box set, ISBN: 978-1-58958-087-9

A series of lectures delivered at BYU by a wide and exciting array of the finest gospel scholars in the Church. Get valuable insights from foremost authorities including General authorities, BYU Professors and Church Educational System instructors. No gospel library will be complete without this valuable resource. Anyone interested in knowing what the top gospel scholars in the Church are saying about such important subjects as historiography, geography, and faith in Christ will be sure to enjoy this handsome box set. This is the perfect gift for any student of the Book of Mormon.

Contributors include: Neal A. Maxwell, Boyd K. Packer, Jeffrey R. Holland, Russell M. Nelson, Dallin H. Oaks, Gerald N. Lund, Dean L. Larsen, Joseph Fielding McConkie, Richard Neitzel Holzapfel, Truman G. Madsen, John W. Welch, Robert J. Matthews, Daniel H. Ludlow, Stephen D. Ricks, Grant Underwood, Robert L. Millet, Susan Easton Black, H. Donl Peterson, John L. Sorenson, Monte S. Nyman, Daniel C. Peterson, Stephen E. Robinson, Carolyn J. Rasmus, Dennis L. Largey, C. Max Caldwell, Andrew C. Skinner, S. Michael Wilcox, Paul R. Cheesman, K. Douglas Bassett, Douglas E. Brinley, Richard O. Cowan, Donald W. Parry, Bruce A. Van Orden, Kenneth W. Anderson, Leland Gentry, S. Kent Brown, H. Dean Garrett, Lee L. Donaldson, Robert E. Parsons, S. Brent Farley, Rodney Turner, Larry E. Dahl, Mae Blanch, Rex C. Reeve Jr., E. Dale LeBaron, Clyde J. Williams, Chauncey C. Riddle, Kent P. Jackson, Daniel K. Judd, Neal E. Lambert, Michael W. Middleton, R. Wayne Shute, John M. Butler, and many more!

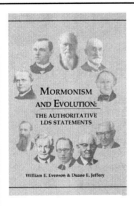

Mormonism and Evolution: The Authoritative LDS Statements

Edited by William E. Evenson and Duane E. Jeffrey

Paperback, ISBN: 978-1-58958-093-0

The Church of Jesus Christ of Latter-day Saints (the Mormon Church) has generally been viewed by the public as anti-evolutionary in its doctrine and teachings. But official statements on the subject by the Church's highest governing quorum and/or president have been considerably more open and diverse than is popularly believed.

This book compiles in full all known authoritative statements (either authored or formally approved for publication) by the Church's highest leaders on the topics of evolution and the origin of human beings. The editors provide historical context for these statements that allows the reader to see what stimulated the issuing of each particular document and how they stand in relation to one another.

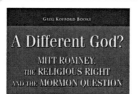

A Different God?
Mitt Romney the Religious Right
and the Mormon Question

Craig L. Foster

Paperback, ISBN: 978-1-58958-117-3

In the contested terrain of American politics, nowhere is the conflict more intense, even brutal, than in the territory of public life also claimed by religion. Mitt Romney's 2007–08 presidential campaign is a textbook example.

Religious historian (and ardent Republican) Craig L. Foster revisits that campaign with an astute focus on the never-quite-contained hostility that Romney triggered among America's religious right. Although few political campaign are known for their kindness, the back-stabbing, mean-spirited attacks, eruptions of irrationalism, and downright lies exploded into one of the meanest chapters of recent American political history.

Foster readjusts rosy views of America as the tolerant, pluralistic society against the context of its lengthy, colorful, and bruising history of religious discrimination and oppression against many religious groups, among them Mormonism. Mormons are now respected and admired--although the image hasn't tilted enough to work for Romney instead of against him. Their turbulent past of suspicion, marginalization, physical violence, and being deprived of voting rights has sometimes made them, in turn, suspicious, hostile, and politically naive. How much of this pattern of mutual name-calling stems from theology and how much from theocratic ideals?

Foster appraises Romney's success and strengths—and also places where he stumbled, analyzing an intriguing pattern of "what-ifs?" of policy, personality, and positioning. But perhaps even more intriguing is the anti-Romney campaign launched by a divided and fragmenting religious right who pulled together in a rare show of unity to chill a Mormon's presidential aspirations. What does Romney's campaign and the resistance of the religious right mean for America in the twenty-first century?

In this meticulously researched, comprehensively documented, and passionately argued analysis of a still-ongoing campaign, Craig Foster poses questions that go beyond both Romney and the religious right to engage the soul of American politics.

Penny Tracts and Polemics: A Critical Analysis of Anti-Mormon Pamphleteering in Great Britain, 1837–1860

Craig L. Foster

Hardcover, ISBN: 978-1-58958-005-3

By 1860, Mormonism had enjoyed a presence in Great Britain for over twenty years. Mormon missionaries experienced unprecedented success in conversions and many new converts had left Britain's shores for a new life and a new religion in the far western mountains of the American continent.

With the success of the Mormons came tales of duplicity, priestcraft, sexual seduction, and uninhibited depravity among the new religious adherents. Thousands of pamphlets were sold or given to the British populace as a way of discouraging people from joining the Mormon Church. Foster places the creation of these English anti-Mormon pamphlets in their historical context. He discusses the authors, the impact of the publications and the Mormon response. With illustrations and detailed bibliography.

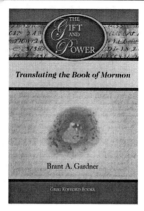

The Gift and Power: Translating the Book of Mormon

Brant A. Gardner

Hardcover, ISBN: 978-1-58958-131-9

From Brant A. Gardner, the author of the highly praised *Second Witness* commentaries on the Book of Mormon, comes *The Gift and Power: Translating the Book of Mormon*. In this first book-length treatment of the translation process, Gardner closely examines the accounts surrounding Joseph Smith's translation of the Book of Mormon to answer a wide spectrum of questions about the process, including: Did the Prophet use seerstones common to folk magicians of his time? How did he use them? And, what is the relationship to the golden plates and the printed text?

Approaching the topic in three sections, part 1 examines the stories told about Joseph, folk magic, and the translation. Part 2 examines the available evidence to determine how closely the English text replicates the original plate text. And part 3 seeks to explain how seer stones worked, why they no longer work, and how Joseph Smith could have produced a translation with them.

Second Witness: Analytical and Contextual Commentatry on the Book of Mormon

Brant A. Gardner

Second Witness, a new six-volume series from Greg Kofford Books, takes a detailed, verse-by-verse look at the Book of Mormon. It marshals the best of modern scholarship and new insights into a consistent picture of the Book of Mormon as a historical document. Taking a faithful but scholarly approach to the text and reading it through the insights of linguistics, anthropology, and ethnohistory, the commentary approaches the text from a variety of perspectives: how it was created, how it relates to history and culture, and what religious insights it provides.

The commentary accepts the best modern scholarship, which focuses on a particular region of Mesoamerica as the most plausible location for the Book of Mormon's setting. For the first time, that location—its peoples, cultures, and historical trends—are used as the backdrop for reading the text. The historical background is not presented as proof, but rather as an explanatory context.

The commentary does not forget Mormon's purpose in writing. It discusses the doctrinal and theological aspects of the text and highlights the way in which Mormon created it to meet his goal of "convincing . . . the Jew and Gentile that Jesus is the Christ, the Eternal God."

Praise for the *Second Witness* series:

"Gardner not only provides a unique tool for understanding the Book of Mormon as an ancient document written by real, living prophets, but he sets a standard for Latter-day Saint thinking and writing about scripture, providing a model for all who follow. . . . No other reference source will prove as thorough and valuable for serious readers of the Book of Mormon."

-Neal A. Maxwell Institute, Brigham Young University

1. 1st Nephi: 978-1-58958-041-1
2. 2nd Nephi–Jacob: 978-1-58958-042-8
3. Enos–Mosiah: 978-1-58958-043-5
4. Alma: 978-1-58958-044-2
5. Helaman–3rd Nephi: 978-1-58958-045-9
6. 4th Nephi–Moroni: 978-1-58958-046-6

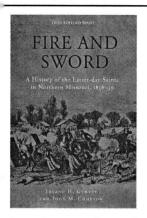

Fire and Sword: A History of the Latter-day Saints in Northern Missouri, 1836-39

Leland Homer Gentry and Todd M. Compton

Hardcover, ISBN: 978-1-58958-103-6

Many Mormon dreams flourished in Missouri. So did many Mormon nightmares.

The Missouri period—especially from the summer of 1838 when Joseph took over vigorous, personal direction of this new Zion until the spring of 1839 when he escaped after five months of imprisonment—represents a moment of intense crisis in Mormon history. Representing the greatest extremes of devotion and violence, commitment and intolerance, physical suffering and terror—mobbings, battles, massacres, and political "knockdowns"—it shadowed the Mormon psyche for a century.

Leland Gentry was the first to step beyond this disturbing period as a one-sided symbol of religious persecution and move toward understanding it with careful documentation and evenhanded analysis. In Fire and Sword, Todd Compton collaborates with Gentry to update this foundational work with four decades of new scholarship, more insightful critical theory, and the wealth of resources that have become electronically available in the last few years.

Compton gives full credit to Leland Gentry's extraordinary achievement, particularly in documenting the existence of Danites and in attempting to tell the Missourians' side of the story; but he also goes far beyond it, gracefully drawing into the dialogue signal interpretations written since Gentry and introducing the raw urgency of personal writings, eyewitness journalists, and bemused politicians seesawing between human compassion and partisan harshness. In the lush Missouri landscape of the Mormon imagination where Adam and Eve had walked out of the garden and where Adam would return to preside over his posterity, the towering religious creativity of Joseph Smith and clash of religious stereotypes created a swift and traumatic frontier drama that changed the Church.

"Swell Suffering":
A Biography of Maurine Whipple

Veda Tebbs Hale

Paperback, ISBN: 978-1-58958-124-1
Hardcover, ISBN: 978-1-58958-122-7

Maurine Whipple, author of what some critics consider Mormonism's greatest novel, *The Giant Joshua,* is an enigma. Her prize-winning novel has never been out of print, and its portrayal of the founding of St. George draws on her own family history to produce its unforgettable and candid portrait of plural marriage's challenges. Yet Maurine's life is full of contradictions and unanswered questions. Veda Tebbs Hale, a personal friend of the paradoxical novelist, answers these questions with sympathy and tact, nailing each insight down with thorough research in Whipple's vast but under-utilized collected papers.

Praise for *"Swell Suffering"*:

"Hale achieves an admirable balance of compassion and objectivity toward an author who seemed fated to offend those who offered to love or befriend her. . . . Readers of this biography will be reminded that Whipple was a full peer of such Utah writers as Virginia Sorensen, Fawn Brodie, and Juanita Brooks, all of whom achieved national fame for their literary and historical works during the mid-twentieth century"
—Levi S. Peterson, author of *The Backslider* and *Juanita Brooks: Mormon Historian*

Modern Polygamy and Mormon Fundamentalism: The Generations after the Manifesto

Brian C. Hales

Paperback, ISBN: 978-1-58958-109-8

Winner of the John Whitmer Historical Association's Smith-Pettit Best Book Award

This fascinating study seeks to trace the historical tapestry that is early Mormon polygamy, details the official discontinuation of the practice by the Church, and, for the first time, describes the many zeal-driven organizations that arose in the wake of that decision. Among the polygamous groups discussed are the LeBaronites, whose "blood atonement" killings sent fear throughout Mormon communities in the late seventies and the eighties; the FLDS Church, which made news recently over its construction of a compound and temple in Texas (Warren Jeffs, the leader of that church, is now standing trial on two felony counts after his being profiled on America's Most Wanted resulted in his capture); and the Allred and Kingston groups, two major factions with substantial membership statistics both in and out of the United States. All these fascinating histories, along with those of the smaller independent groups, are examined and explained in a way that all can appreciate.

Praise for *Modern Polygamy and Mormon Fundamentalism*:

"This book is the most thorough and comprehensive study written on the sugbject to date, providing readers with a clear, candid, and broad sweeping overview of the history, teachings, and practices of modern fundamentalist groups."
— Alexander L. Baugh, Associate Professor of Church History and Doctrine, Brigham Young University

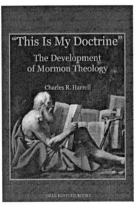

"This is My Doctrine": The Development of Mormon Theology

Charles R. Harrell

Hardcover, ISBN: 978-1-58958-103-6

The principal doctrines defining Mormonism today often bear little resemblance to those it started out with in the early 1830s. This book shows that these doctrines did not originate in a vacuum but were rather prompted and informed by the religious culture from which Mormonism arose. Early Mormons, like their early Christian and even earlier Israelite predecessors, brought with them their own varied culturally conditioned theological presuppositions (a process of convergence) and only later acquired a more distinctive theological outlook (a process of differentiation).

In this first-of-its-kind comprehensive treatment of the development of Mormon theology, Charles Harrell traces the history of Latter-day Saint doctrines from the times of the Old Testament to the present. He describes how Mormonism has carried on the tradition of the biblical authors, early Christians, and later Protestants in reinterpreting scripture to accommodate new theological ideas while attempting to uphold the integrity and authority of the scriptures. In the process, he probes three questions: How did Mormon doctrines develop? What are the scriptural underpinnings of these doctrines? And what do critical scholars make of these same scriptures? In this enlightening study, Harrell systematically peels back the doctrinal accretions of time to provide a fresh new look at Mormon theology.

"*This Is My Doctrine*" will provide those already versed in Mormonism's theological tradition with a new and richer perspective of Mormon theology. Those unacquainted with Mormonism will gain an appreciation for how Mormon theology fits into the larger Jewish and Christian theological traditions.

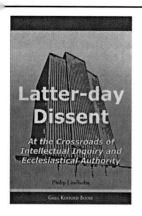

Latter-Day Dissent:
At the Crossroads of Intellectual
Inquiry and Ecclesiastical Authority

Philip Lindholm

Paperback, ISBN: 978-1-58958-128-9

This volume collects, for the first time in book form, stories from the "September Six," a group of intellectuals officially excommunicated or disfellowshipped from the LDS Church in September of 1993 on charges of "apostasy" or "conduct unbecoming" Church members. Their experiences are significant and yet are largely unknown outside of scholarly or more liberal Mormon circles, which is surprising given that their story was immediately propelled onto screens and cover pages across the Western world.

Interviews by Dr. Philip Lindholm (Ph.D. Theology, University of Oxford) include those of the "September Six," Lynne Kanavel Whitesides, Paul James Toscano, Maxine Hanks, Lavina Fielding Anderson, and D. Michael Quinn; as well as Janice Merrill Allred, Margaret Merrill Toscano, Thomas W. Murphy, and former employee of the LDS Church's Public Affairs Department, Donald B. Jessee.

Each interview illustrates the tension that often exists between the Church and its intellectual critics, and highlights the difficulty of accommodating congregational diversity while maintaining doctrinal unity—a difficulty hearkening back to the very heart of ancient Christianity.

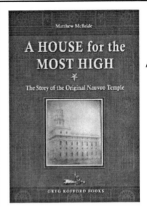

A House for the Most High: The Story of the Original Nauvoo Temple

Matthew McBride

Hardcover, ISBN: 978-1-58958-016-9

This awe-inspiring book is a tribute to the perseverance of the human spirit. *A House for the Most High* is a groundbreaking work from beginning to end with its faithful and comprehensive documentation of the Nauvoo Temple's conception. The behind-the-scenes stories of those determined Saints involved in the great struggle to raise the sacred edifice bring a new appreciation to all readers. McBride's painstaking research now gives us access to valuable first-hand accounts that are drawn straight from the newspaper articles, private diaries, journals, and letters of the steadfast participants.

The opening of this volume gives the reader an extraordinary window into the early temple-building labors of the besieged Church of Jesus Christ of Latter-day Saints, the development of what would become temple-related doctrines in the decade prior to the Nauvoo era, and the 1839 advent of the Saints in Illinois. The main body of this fascinating history covers the significant years, starting from 1840, when this temple was first considered, to the temple's early destruction by a devastating natural disaster. A well-thought-out conclusion completes the epic by telling of the repurchase of the temple lot by the Church in 1937, the lot's excavation in 1962, and the grand announcement in 1999 that the temple would indeed be rebuilt. Also included are an astonishing appendix containing rare and fascinating eyewitness descriptions of the temple and a bibliography of all major source materials. Mormons and non-Mormons alike will discover, within the pages of this book, a true sense of wonder and gratitude for a determined people whose sole desire was to build a sacred and holy temple for the worship of their God.

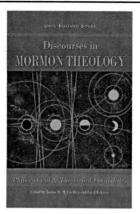

Discourses in Mormon Theology:
Philosophical and Theological
Possibilities

Edited by
James M. McLachlan and Loyd Ericson

Hardcover, ISBN: 978-1-58958-103-6

A mere two hundred years old, Mormonism is still in its infancy compared to other theological disciplines (Judaism, Catholicism, Buddhism, etc.). This volume will introduce its reader to the rich blend of theological viewpoints that exist within Mormonism. The essays break new ground in Mormon studies by exploring the vast expanse of philosophical territory left largely untouched by traditional approaches to Mormon theology. It presents philosophical and theological essays by many of the finest minds associated with Mormonism in an organized and easy-to-understand manner and provides the reader with a window into the fascinating diversity amongst Mormon philosophers. Open-minded students of pure religion will appreciate this volume's thoughtful inquiries.

These essays were delivered at the first conference of the Society for Mormon Philosophy and Theology. Authors include Grant Underwood, Blake T. Ostler, Dennis Potter, Margaret Merrill Toscano, James E. Faulconer, and Robert L. Millet

Praise for *Discourses in Mormon Theology*:

"In short, *Discourses in Mormon Theology* is an excellent compilation of essays that are sure to feed both the mind and soul. It reminds all of us that beyond the white shirts and ties there exists a universe of theological and moral sensitivity that cries out for study and acclamation."
                    -Jeff Needle, Association for Mormon Letters

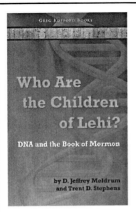

Who Are the Children of Lehi? DNA and the Book of Mormon

D. Jeffrey Meldrum and Trent D. Stephens

Hardcover, ISBN: 978-1-58958-048-0
Paperback, ISBN: 978-1-58958-129-6

How does the Book of Mormon, keystone of the LDS faith, stand up to data about DNA sequencing that puts the ancestors of modern Native Americans in northeast Asia instead of Palestine?

In *Who Are the Children of Lehi?* Meldrum and Stephens examine the merits and the fallacies of DNA-based interpretations that challenge the Book of Mormon's historicity. They provide clear guides to the science, summarize the studies, illuminate technical points with easy-to-grasp examples, and spell out the data's implications.

The results? There is no straight-line conclusion between DNA evidence and "Lamanites." The Book of Mormon's validity lies beyond the purview of scientific empiricism—as it always has. And finally, inspiringly, they affirm Lehi's kinship as one of covenant, not genes.

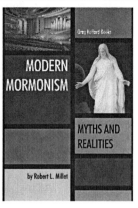

Modern Mormonism: Myths and Realities

Robert L. Millet

Paperback, ISBN: 978-1-58958-127-2

What answer may a Latter-day Saint make to accusations from those of other faiths that "Mormons aren't Christians," or "You think God is a man," and "You worship a different Jesus"? Not only are these charges disconcerting, but the hostility with which they are frequently hurled is equally likely to catch Latter-day Saints off guard.

Now Robert L. Millet, veteran of hundreds of such verbal battles, cogently, helpfully, and scripturally provides important clarifications for Latter-day Saints about eleven of the most frequent myths used to discredit the Church. Along the way, he models how to conduct such a Bible based discussion respectfully, weaving in enlightenment from LDS scriptures and quotations from religious figures in other faiths, ranging from the early church fathers to the archbishop of Canterbury.

Millet enlivens this book with personal experiences as a boy growing up in an area where Mormons were a minuscule and not particularly welcome minority, in one-on-one conversations with men of faith who believed differently, and with his own BYU students who also had lessons to learn about interfaith dialogue. He pleads for greater cooperation in dealing with the genuine moral and social evils afflicting the world, and concludes with his own ardent and reverent testimony of the Savior.

Exploring Mormon Thought Series

Blake T. Ostler

IN VOLUME ONE, *The Attributes of God*, Blake T. Ostler explores Christian and Mormon notions about God. ISBN: 978-1-58958-003-9

IN VOLUME TWO, *The Problems of Theism and the Love of God*, Blake Ostler explores issues related to soteriology, or the theory of salvation. ISBN: 978-1-58958-095-4

IN VOLUME THREE, *Of God and Gods*, Ostler analyzes and responds to the arguments of contemporary international theologians, reconstructs and interprets Joseph Smith's important King Follett Discourse and Sermon in the Grove, and argues persuasively for the Mormon doctrine of "robust deification." ISBN: 978-1-58958-107-4

Praise for the *Exploring Mormon Thought* series:

"These books are the most important works on Mormon theology ever written. There is nothing currently available that is even close to the rigor and sophistication of these volumes. B. H. Roberts and John A. Widtsoe may have had interesting insights in the early part of the twentieth century, but they had neither the temperament nor the training to give a rigorous defense of their views in dialogue with a wider stream of Christian theology. Sterling McMurrin and Truman Madsen had the capacity to engage Mormon theology at this level, but neither one did."

—Neal A. Maxwell Institute, Brigham Young University

Hugh Nibley:
A Consecrated Life

Boyd Jay Petersen

Hardcover, ISBN: 978-1-58958-019-0

Winner of the Mormon History Association's Best Biography Award

As one of the LDS Church's most widely recognized scholars, Hugh Nibley is both an icon and an enigma. Through complete access to Nibley's correspondence, journals, notes, and papers, Petersen has painted a portrait that reveals the man behind the legend.

Starting with a foreword written by Zina Nibley Petersen and finishing with appendices that include some of the best of Nibley's personal correspondence, the biography reveals aspects of the tapestry of the life of one who has truly consecrated his life to the service of the Lord.

Praise for *A Consecrated Life*:

"Hugh Nibley is generally touted as one of Mormonism's greatest minds and perhaps its most prolific scholarly apologist. Just as hefty as some of Nibley's largest tomes, this authorized biography is delightfully accessible and full of the scholar's delicious wordplay and wit, not to mention some astonishing war stories and insights into Nibley's phenomenal acquisition of languages. Introduced by a personable foreword from the author's wife (who is Nibley's daughter), the book is written with enthusiasm, respect and insight. . . . On the whole, Petersen is a careful scholar who provides helpful historical context. . . . This project is far from hagiography. It fills an important gap in LDS history and will appeal to a wide Mormon audience."

—Publishers Weekly

"Well written and thoroughly researched, Petersen's biography is a must-have for anyone struggling to reconcile faith and reason."

—Greg Taggart, Association for Mormon Letters

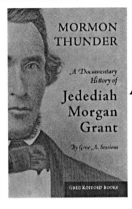

Mormon Thunder: A Documentary History of Jedediah Morgan Grant

Gene A. Sessions

Paperback, ISBN: 978-1-58958-111-1

Jedediah Morgan Grant was a man who knew no compromise when it came to principles—and his principles were clearly representative, argues Gene A. Sessions, of Mormonism's first generation. His life is a glimpse of a Mormon world whose disappearance coincided with the death of this "pious yet rambunctiously radical preacher, flogging away at his people, demanding otherworldliness and constant sacrifice." It was "an eschatological, premillennial world in which every individual teetered between salvation and damnation and in which unsanitary privies and appropriating a stray cow held the same potential for eternal doom as blasphemy and adultery."

Updated and newly illustrated with more photographs, this second edition of the award-winning documentary history (first published in 1982) chronicles Grant's ubiquitous role in the Mormon history of the 1840s and '50s. In addition to serving as counselor to Brigham Young during two tumultuous and influential years at the end of his life, he also portentously befriended Thomas L. Kane, worked to temper his unruly brother-in-law William Smith, captained a company of emigrants into the Salt Lake Valley in 1847, and journeyed to the East on several missions to bolster the position of the Mormons during the crises surrounding the runaway judges affair and the public revelation of polygamy.

Jedediah Morgan Grant's voice rises powerfully in these pages, startling in its urgency in summoning his people to sacrifice and moving in its tenderness as he communicated to his family. From hastily scribbled letters to extemporaneous sermons exhorting obedience, and the notations of still stunned listeners, the sound of "Mormon Thunder" rolls again in "a boisterous amplification of what Mormonism really was, and would never be again."

Hearken, O Ye People:
The Historical Setting of Joseph Smith's Ohio Revelations

Mark Lyman Staker

Hardcover, ISBN: 978-1-58958-113-5

2010 Best Book Award - John Whitmer Historical Association

2011 Best Book Award - Mormon History Association

More of Mormonism's canonized revelations originated in or near Kirtland than any other place. Yet many of the events connected with those revelations and their 1830s historical context have faded over time. Mark Staker reconstructs the cultural experiences by which Kirtland's Latter-day Saints made sense of the revelations Joseph Smith pronounced. This volume rebuilds that exciting decade using clues from numerous archives, privately held records, museum collections, and even the soil where early members planted corn and homes. From this vast array of sources he shapes a detailed narrative of weather, religious backgrounds, dialect differences, race relations, theological discussions, food preparation, frontier violence, astronomical phenomena, and myriad daily customs of nineteenth-century life. The result is a "from the ground up" experience that today's Latter-day Saints can all but walk into and touch.

Praise for *Hearken O Ye People*:

"I am not aware of a more deeply researched and richly contextualized study of any period of Mormon church history than Mark Staker's study of Mormons in Ohio. We learn about everything from the details of Alexander Campbell's views on priesthood authority to the road conditions and weather on the four Lamanite missionaries' journey from New York to Ohio. All the Ohio revelations and even the First Vision are made to pulse with new meaning. This book sets a new standard of in-depth research in Latter-day Saint history."

-Richard Bushman, author of *Joseph Smith: Rough Stone Rolling*

"To be well-informed, any student of Latter-day Saint history and doctrine must now be acquainted with the remarkable research of Mark Staker on the important history of the church in the Kirtland, Ohio, area."

-Neal A. Maxwell Institute, Brigham Young University

"Let the Earth Bring Forth"
Evolution and Scripture

Howard C. Stutz

Paperback, ISBN: 978-1-58958-126-5

A century ago in 1809, Charles Darwin was born. Fifty years later, he published a scientific treatise describing the process of speciation that launched what appeared to be a challenge to the traditional religious interpretation of how life was created on earth. The controversy has erupted anew in the last decade as Creationists and Young Earth adherents challenge school curricula and try to displace "the theory of evolution."

This book is filled with fascinating examples of speciation by the well-known process of mutation but also by the less well-known processes of sexual recombination and polyploidy. In addition to the fossil record, Howard Stutz examines the evidence from the embryo stages of human beings and other creatures to show how selection and differentiation moved development in certain favored directions while leaving behind evidence of earlier, discarded developments. Anatomy, biochemistry, and genetics are all examined in their turn.

With rigorously scientific clarity but in language accessible to a popular audience, the book proceeds to its conclusion, reached after a lifetime of study: the divine map of creation is one supported by both scientific evidence and the scriptures. This is a book to be read, not only for its fascinating scientific insights, but also for a new appreciation of well-known scriptures.

CPSIA information can be obtained
at www.ICGtesting.com
Printed in the USA
FSOW02n2142271116
27886FS